CHANCERY LANE

'The Strong box of the Empire'

Aidan Lawes

PRO Publications

PRO Publications
Public Record Office
Ruskin Avenue
Kew
Surrey
TW9 4DU

© Crown Copyright 1996
ISBN 1 873162 35 X

CONTENTS

ILLUSTRATIONS

꩜꩜꩜꩜꩜꩜꩜꩜꩜꩜꩜꩜꩜꩜꩜꩜꩜꩜꩜꩜

The decorated capitals with which each chapter begins are all taken from the *Report of the Lords Committees Appointed ... To View and Consider the Publick Records* (1719).

The pictograms between pages 1-12 are mainly taken from Sir Francis Palgrave's *Antient Kalendars and Inventories* (1836).

The sketches of staff and readers between pages 46-53, some clearly written in ink on document ordering tickets by staff on duty in the reading rooms, are from PRO 8/63.

Frontispiece 'The Storehouse of the Nation's Records', from *The Daily Graphic* in 1896.

Preface

The full story of the housing of the public records since the twelfth century tends to be a repetitive cycle of deteriorating or inadequate buildings, delay, repair or removal, further decay, and so on, wearisome in its telling.

E M Hallam and M Roper "The Capital and the Records of the Nation", *London Journal* Vol.4, no.1, 1978.

The old correspondence is full of personalities which I should not care to put at the disposal of any irresponsible writer, who might, for instance, like to publish a comic history of the office.

Deputy Keeper A E Stamp to M S Giuseppi, Head of Search Department, 1 June 1933, quoted in J Cantwell *The Public Record Office, 1838-1958.*

The Public Record Office (PRO) building which dominates Chancery Lane will close its doors to readers of original records in December 1996 after 140 years of service. The association of the site with the public records goes back much further however to at least 1377, when the Chancery official responsible for record-keeping, the Master of the Rolls, took over what subsequently became known as the Rolls Estate. We could not let this occasion pass without acknowledgement and this little booklet is intended to give a brief illustrated history of the site; its denizens, staff and readers; and the tale of the housing of the public records over 600 years. While not a comic history, the voices of personalities, officials and users, will, it is hoped, relieve the more wearisome aspects of the story. Those curious to investigate further are referred to the Select Bibliography.

This account concludes in 1977, when the new Record Office at Kew first opened its doors to the public, although there is a brief mention of Chancery Lane's closure and the transfer of its records to the now extended Kew site. The period 1977-1996 saw many developments, not least the Office's transition to Executive Agency status, its increasing emphasis on reader services and the problems and opportunities afforded by the information technology revolution. This belongs to the future, not the past, and is a period too significant for the necessarily cursory treatment it would have received here. Interested parties are referred to the *Annual Reports* of the Keeper for these years. There are those who have compared the PRO to a dinosaur, an essentially nineteenth-century institution, incapable of adjustment to late twentieth-century conditions. To those who read these pages it should become clear that evolution has been, and still is, continuous.

It owes much to the work of Elizabeth Hallam Smith and Jack Cantwell, published and unpublished, and to the endeavours of the Publishing Team, not least to Melvyn Stainton's design sense and the patience of Millie Skinns.

'The Storehouse of the Nation's Records', 1895

Records and Repositories, 1100-1700

Early Record Keeping Practice

he key written records of central government were, from earliest times, kept with the royal treasure and jewels and regarded as of equal importance. They were stored in the king's castle at Winchester, the Anglo-Saxon capital, or accompanied the king on those itinerant royal progresses through the kingdom that were so essential to the maintenance of control. Certainly our oldest surviving public record, Domesday Book, William the Conqueror's sweeping survey of landholding and tax liability commissioned in 1085, was originally kept at Winchester and known at that time as the 'Book of Winchester'.

As bureaucracy developed and the number of records multiplied, departments of state, such as the king's chancery and the courts of law, ceased automatically to follow the royal household and came to settle at Westminster, often making use of the secure storage provided by local religious houses for their records; Westminster Abbey, St. Bartholomew's Priory in Smithfield and the New Temple all served this purpose. English monasteries could also be required to supply the King with a sumpter (pack) horse for carrying the records of Chancery from place to place. On 14 October 1296 for example, a writ was issued to the abbot of Waverley in Surrey, ordering him to send a strong horse to the royal chancery, then at Bury St. Edmunds where Parliament was meeting, to transport the rolls of Chancery (C 255/ 9/1 no. 32).

The Public Record Office possesses a number of medieval storage chests designed for the secure accommodation and transport of records. A typical example reproduced as fig 1 (E 27 no. 7) is a pine chest of the fourteenth century, plated with iron, with hasps for padlocks, rings at the ends for ease of transport and little feet to raise the chest off damp floors. Inside chests such as these were smaller wooden chests, some known as 'pixes', or

Fig.1 Fourteenth-century
Iron-bound Chest E 27/case 7

Fig.2 A hamper

Fig.3 A skippet

hampers of woven twigs. Wooden or metal skippets protected precious seals. Small rolls of parchment might be held together in white leather pouches, some of which still contain Exchequer accounts.

Records were the responsibility of the officials who created them and each made their own arrangements for storage, if indeed they saw fit to keep them at all. Not until the nineteenth century was a single central repository established.

Westminster Abbey and the Treasury of the Receipt

The most important monastic record repositories were the Chapel of the Pyx and the undercroft of the Chapter House of Westminster Abbey, largely used by the Treasury of the Wardrobe and the Exchequer, the main department of finance, to house the royal jewels and plate, the standard coinage of the realm, treaties with foreign states and other documents such as Domesday Book.

An early finding aid for records held by a pre-cursor of the Public Record Office known as the Treasury of the Receipt, *Liber A* and *Liber B* (E 36/274-275), was compiled c. 1292, using pictograms as a means of rapidly identifying relevant documents not unlike the present international use of icons on computer screens. Documents were then classified by country and appropriately labelled: Aragon was represented by jousting knights, Gascony by grape-treading, Wales by an archer.

After the Dissolution of the Monasteries in the sixteenth century and the dispersal of Westminster's monastic community, the main body of the Chapter House effectively became a redundant building and was

Fig. 4 Section of the Chapter House, Westminster Abbey in the early nineteenth- century MPB 2/99/1

eventually reconstructed with a mezzanine floor inserted to allow it to be shelved for record storage up to the very roof (fig 4). By the eighteenth century it was the most important record office for both the Exchequer and the Courts of King's Bench and Common Pleas. Most of the records were removed to the Public Record Office in 1857-59, although the Chapel of the Pyx was not finally cleared until 1911.

The Tower of London

The Tower of London offered an even more secure repository for both treasure and records, used by Chancery, Treasury and Wardrobe. In the fourteenth century it became the main repository for Chancery records, although most regular transfers had ceased by c. 1500 when the Rolls Chapel took over this role for such records from the reign of Richard III onwards. Both the White Tower (see fig 5) and the Wakefield Tower housed records, the former also being used for the storage of gunpowder. By 1712 it was full and pressure had to be put on the Board of Ordnance for extra space to house the records of Chancery suits. The Tower remained a

In cophino ligneo ad tale signū.

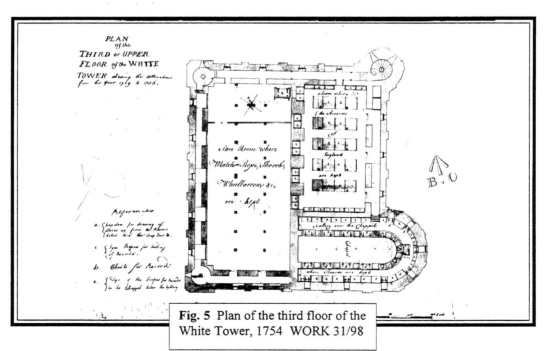

Fig. 5 Plan of the third floor of the White Tower, 1754 WORK 31/98

record office until 1856 when its records were transferred to the new repository in Chancery Lane. Fire had been an ever-present danger. In 1788, only a change in wind direction had saved the records from the same fate that befell many Irish medieval records stored in similar circumstances in Dublin Castle.

It was at the Tower that the first general attempt at systematic reorganisation of the Exchequer records took place under Walter Stapledon, Bishop of Exeter and Treasurer of England between 1320 and 1322. Documents were ferried there from the Westminster repository for cataloguing and then returned. A catalogue of diplomatic and other documents was drawn up, also using pictograms.

The pictograms illustrated in this section are all taken from the printed version of Stapledon's calendar (E 36/268) or other medieval finding aids published in Sir Francis Palgrave's *Antient Kalendars and Inventories* (1836).

Not until the seventeenth century was systematic cataloguing with the antiquarian researcher in mind undertaken, although in 1601 the record keeper, William Lambarde, presented Queen Elizabeth I in the Tower with his *Pandect* or guide to the records there. When William Prynne took over the office of Keeper of the Records in the Tower at the Restoration he reported that the records were in a 'deplorable pickle .. overspread with dust, cobwebs and eaten up with rust, cankers, moths, worms, in their over-much neglected cells'. In a letter to Sir Harbottle Grimstone he complained 'I have almost been choked with the dust of neglected Records (interred in their own rubbish for sundry years) in the White Tower, their rust eating out the tops of my gloves with their touch, and their dust rendering me twice a day as black as a Chymney Sweeper; I have at last tumbled them all over, and distributed them into sundry indigested heaps, which I intend God willing to reduce into order by degrees'. Anthony Wood's diary for June 1667 records a visit to the Tower Record Office where Prynne provided him with a desk in the Wakefield Tower, sitting next to William Dugdale, author of the *Monasticon Anglicanum*. Opening hours at the Record Office were then 7 a.m. to 11 a.m. and 1 p.m. to 5 p.m., but 8 a.m. to 4 p.m. in winter. A general guide to the repositories at Westminster, the Tower and the Rolls Chapel was published in 1622:

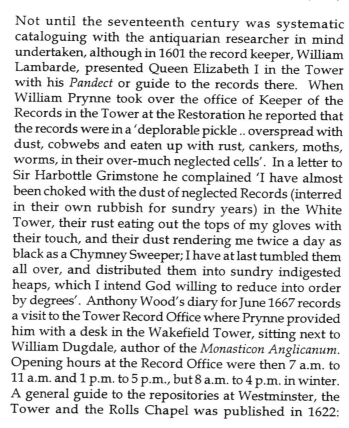

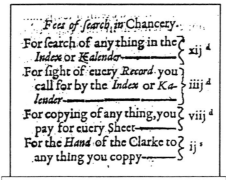

Fig. 6 Thomas Powell's *Direction for Search of Records* (1622)

Thomas Powell's *Direction for Search of Records* which was essentially aimed at lawyers.

At this period the Keeper of the Records and his clerks derived most of their income from fees. So much depended on customer satisfaction that, in some cases, if the relevant document could not be found an appropriate forgery might be supplied. In 1674, one William Thompson, an apprentice clerk, forged a  document for a searcher called Peter Atkinson. The discovery of this is recorded with horror in the Fee Book of the Tower Record Office (OBS 1/672). The standard search fee of 10 shillings should be compared to the average daily wage of the private soldier of one shilling.

Fig. 7 Tower Record Office Fee Book - 1674 OBS 1/672

Enrolment and Users

The King's secretariat, Chancery, which issued all Royal Letters and Writs, does not appear to have systematically kept copies of documents issued under the Great Seal of the kingdom until c.1200 when King John's Chancellor, Hubert Walter, began to keep copies in a closely written and abbreviated form of Latin on parchment skins, sewn head to tail to form long rolls that could be compactly and economically stored. These enrolments were the medieval equivalent of microfilm and suffered many of the same disadvantages of that medium, not least in the need to laboriously scroll through from beginning to end to find the entry you want. One of these early series, the Patent Rolls in the record class C 66 is still being added to today, although now in book form.

The Exchequer appears to have started systematic enrolment of its audit of accounts with the sheriffs, royal officials who were responsible for collecting and disbursing the crown's revenues in the shire counties, much earlier. The earliest such enrolment, or pipe roll, survives from 1129-30. The parchment skins that formed Exchequer enrolments were sewn at the head of the skin, rather than in one continuous roll, presenting rather different problems of storage and consultation.

The Plea Rolls of the central law courts also survive from the late twelfth century and those of King's Bench and the Court of Common Pleas run in continuous series from the thirteenth century to the nineteenth century.

Most early users had a business purpose behind their researches. Religious houses came looking for evidence of royal grants missing from their own archives, such as the prior of Holy Trinity Aldgate who used Chancery enrolments to prove that he was entitled to close a certain road in 1276. There were landowners who needed to trace the descent of a manor or evidence of transfer of title, such as the Welshman George Owen of Henllys who came to London in 1589 to consult "the Book of Domesday which remaineth with Mr Agard and Fenton in the Cellars office .. the book is very ancient and hard to be read and whoso findeth any things must pay for the copy of every line iiij. d and it must be exemplified in the self same correctness as it is written in the book, which is strange and hard for any man to read". Family lawyers came to check Inquisitions Post Mortem. Unsettled debts which were sometimes attached to the lands of the debtor were another popular enquiry. One of the first historians to use the public records was Matthew Paris, the chronicler, at the Exchequer.

Chancery Lane - The Rolls Estate

The House of Converts

 n 1232, the House of Converts or *Domus Conversorum* was established by King Henry III in Chancery Lane (then 'Neustrate') on the site of what later became the Public Record Office. The land had been held by the Templars from the abbot of Westminster and they had built New Street to link the Old Temple in Holborn with the New Temple by the river. In the thirteenth century, the records of the court of Chancery were held in the King's Treasury in the New Temple. The *Domus Conversorum* whose foundation is recorded in the Charter Rolls (C 53/26 m.18) was intended as a refuge for Jews who had converted to Christianity. Here they were to be taught useful trades, rather than usury, and in the chapel attached to the House of Converts they were to learn more about the Christian faith.

 After the expulsion of the Jews from England in 1290, it effectively became a redundant building although the official post of Keeper of the House of Converts remained in being and its funds continued to be used to make pension payments to converted Jews into the eighteenth century.

In 1377, the post of Keeper of the House of Converts was formally annexed to the post of Keeper, or Master, of the Rolls of Chancery. The former post only lapsed in 1873 when a practising Jew, George Jessel, was appointed as Master of the Rolls and it was thought inappropriate to make him also Keeper of the House of Converts. The Master of the Rolls came into possession of the whole site which became known as the Rolls Estate or the Liberty of the Rolls. Part of the site became his private residence and the former chapel of the House of Converts became his private chapel.

Fig. 8 Rolls Chapel as portrayed by Matthew Paris

The Rolls Chapel

In the fourteenth century, the Master of the Rolls began to use the Rolls Estate site for the storage of records, notably those more recent Chancery enrolments that

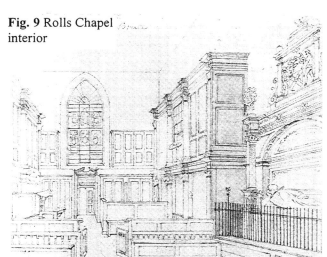

Fig. 9 Rolls Chapel interior

Chancery officials, many of whom were based in and around Chancery Lane, were not ready to dispatch to the more distant "permanent" archive repository of the Tower. The Rolls Chapel itself was pressed into service for records storage and, by the end of the fifteenth

century, had become the main repository for chancery enrolments and the transfer of its records to the Tower ceased. Thus Chancery records from the reign of Richard III onwards came to be housed at the Rolls Chapel and those for earlier periods at the Tower. The medieval chancel of the Rolls Chapel was destroyed in the mid-seventeenth century, possibly in the Great Fire of London, but the Chapel was then reconstructed.

Fig. 10 Demolition of the Rolls Chapel

9

In his diary, Samuel Pepys records attending divine service at the Rolls Chapel, and being disappointed by the quality of the sermon. On 15 March 1669, the diary records his visit there on official duty, to have the records searched: "I hired a clerk there to read to me about twelve or more several rolls which I did call for: and it was great pleasure to me to see the method wherein their Rolles are kept; that when the Master of the Office, one Mr Case, doth call for them .. he did most readily turn to them". At noon, the office shut and Pepys went for a leisurely lunch. He then returned to the Rolls Chapel "and did a little more business", recording at the end of the day his "great content for what I have this day found, having got almost as much as I desire of the history of the Navy from 1618 to 1642".

Record clerks in the Rolls Chapel, and other repositories, often compiled their own private indexes that were regarded as their own personal property and could be sold on to their successors in office, thus the indexes of Henry Rooke were purchased by his successor, John Kipling, and, in turn, by Kipling's successor, Thomas Palmer, whose executors eventually sold them to the Public Record Office where, for many years, they remained in regular use in the Round Room.

Fig.11 Statue of George I from Rolls House.

In 1717, the House of Converts was demolished and replaced by a Palladian residence, designed by Sir Colin Campbell and deemed more suitable for Sir Joseph Jekyll, then Master of the Rolls. The Rolls Chapel remained but was extensively repaired in the 1770s and fitted out with cupboards for record storage. In 1833, the Record Commission reported that the Rolls Chapel "exhibits a most remarkable specimen of the extremist economy of space, the very seats of the chapel being in fact cases for records. On the ground are the Patent Rolls, in a spot so dark that no one can see to read any one there, and a candle is not properly

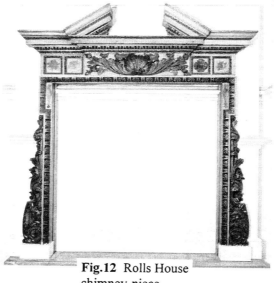

Fig.12 Rolls House chimney-piece

allowed. They can be removed, therefore, only by guess matured into habit!"

Rolls House was demolished in 1895 but two carved wooden chimney-pieces were incorporated into the fabric of the nineteenth century Public Record Office building. One was incongruously mounted half-way up the side of a wall in what eventually became the reader's refreshment room near to the Round reading room on the ground floor. A marble statue of King George I, in ancient Roman costume, later moved to the central entrance lobby of the present building, formerly occupied a niche over the judicial bench of the court in Rolls House. The Rolls Chapel continued its dual function as records store and private chapel until it was also demolished in 1895, although many felt that sufficient medieval features remained to justify its retention and there was a public outcry. All that now remains is the thirteenth-century chancel arch that was re-erected on an external wall in front of an area later used for bicycle racks and rubbish bins; a medieval hall; a number of tomb effigies and stained glass windows showing the arms of various Masters of the Rolls, some dating from the seventeenth century, most added in 1899.

The monuments all reflect its role as the quasi-private chapel of the Master of the Rolls and reflect the

11

Fig.13 Dr John Yonge, Master of the Rolls, died 1516

secularisation of an office that, like most government posts, had been the preserve of clerical administrators in the Middle Ages. The finest, almost certainly by the Renaissance sculptor Pietro Torrigiano, who was responsible for the effigies of Henry VII and his wife in Westminster Abbey, is of Dr John Yonge, Master of the Rolls and dean of York, who died in 1516; but the other two are of laymen with their families, Richard Alington (died 1561), whose brother-in-law was Master of the Rolls, and Lord Bruce of Kinloss (died 1611), Master of the Rolls under James I.

The Public Record Office established a museum on the site of the former chapel in 1902 which attracted a growing number of visitors, rising from 2,951 in 1920 to 10,242 in 1948, sufficiently popular for its threatened closure to be used as a bargaining counter with the Treasury when staff cuts loomed in the early 1950s. The

Fig.14 The Rolls Chapel as a museum

museum closed in 1986 after a major exhibition to mark the 900th anniversary of Domesday Book. It was ultimately reopened as a microfilm reading room for probate records and nonconformist registers, death duty records and state papers.

Records and Repositories, 1500-1838

The State Paper Office

rom the sixteenth century, the records of the Secretaries of State, predecessors of the ministers at the Home Office and Foreign Office, which were not established as government departments until 1782, were kept at the very heart of government in the Palace of Whitehall. What became known as the State Paper Office moved to the Holbein Gate in 1619. So neglected and dilapidated did this building become that it had to be demolished in 1759, at which time sledge-hammers had to be used to batter down the doors of the room housing Privy Council records as no one could find the key.

The State Papers were then dispersed amongst a number of buildings in Whitehall, often in basements liable to flooding. In 1825, a State Paper Commission was established to print and publish the state papers, but not until 1834 was a purpose-built repository, a distinguished classical building designed by Sir John Soane, erected near Green Park. In the 1830s, it attracted about 18 readers a day, all of whom required special permits to see the records. Unrestricted access, and then only to pre-1688 material, was not granted until 1858. After the establishment of the Public Record Office in 1838, it was possible that the State Paper Office would develop into a rival record office for departmental records, with the PRO essentially a repository for legal documents. However, the first Deputy Keeper, Sir Francis Palgrave, persuaded the Treasury to send its records to the PRO rather than the State Paper Office and this was to prove a vital turning point.

The State Paper Commission was wound up in 1854 when the State Paper Office and its staff were absorbed into the new Public Record Office. The building was demolished in 1862 to make way for the new Foreign Office and the state papers were then transferred to the Public Record Office in Chancery Lane. It had been suggested earlier that the state papers and other documents of purely historical interest should be housed by the British Museum, leaving the new Public Record Office only with legal and administrative records, but this was strenuously resisted by the keepers at the Public Record Office.

Parliamentary Enquiries and the Record Commissions

Growing antiquarian interest in records throughout Europe in the seventeenth century culminated in the appointment of a Historiographer Royal, Thomas Rymer, in 1699. Rymer was commissioned to publish an edition of key diplomatic sources and his *Foedera*, which appeared in 20 volumes between 1704 and 1735, was the first large-scale official publication of record sources in this country.

Between 1703 and 1729, the House of Lords appointed a number of committees to examine record-keeping practice and the repositories where the public records were stored. These reports were all printed in their *Journals*. They reveal the serious neglect of the records of defunct courts, such as Star Chamber, Augmentations,

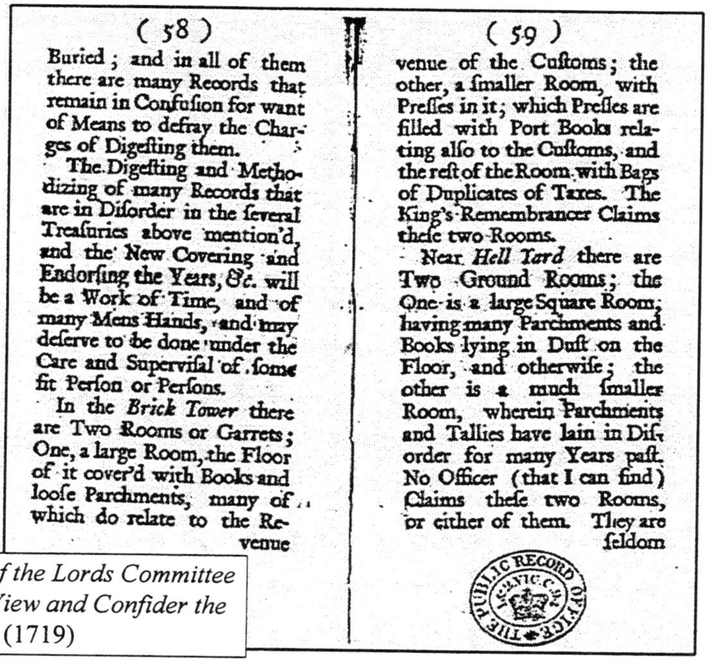

(58)

Buried ; and in all of them there are many Records that remain in Confusion for want of Means to defray the Charges of Digesting them.

The Digesting and Methodizing of many Records that are in Disorder in the several Treasuries above mention'd, and the New Covering and Endorsing the Years, &c. will be a Work of Time, and of many Mens Hands, and may deserve to be done under the Care and Supervisal of some fit Person or Persons.

In the *Brick Tower* there are Two Rooms or Garrets ; One, a large Room, the Floor of it cover'd with Books and loose Parchments, many of which do relate to the Revenue

(59)

venue of the Customs ; the other, a smaller Room, with Presses in it ; which Presses are filled with Port Books relating also to the Customs, and the rest of the Room with Bags of Duplicates of Taxes. The King's Remembrancer Claims these two Rooms.

Near *Hell Yard* there are Two Ground Rooms ; the One is a large Square Room, having many Parchments and Books lying in Dust on the Floor, and otherwise ; the other is a much smaller Room, wherein Parchments and Tallies have lain in Disorder for many Years past. No Officer (that I can find) Claims these two Rooms, or either of them. They are seldom

Fig.15 *Report of the Lords Committee Appointed...To View and Confider the Publick Records* (1719)

15

Wards and Liveries and Requests. In 1709, for example, the records of the Court of Wards were found to be kept in a house adjoining that of the royal fishmonger in Fish Yard, Westminster, and effectively in his custody. Many of these records remain unfit for production to this day. As late as 1830, Ancient Miscellanea of the King's Remembrancer's Department, formerly stored in a great "ark" in Westminster Hall were removed to the King's Mews at Charing Cross, there to become "a mass of

Fig.16 State in which a Roll of the Common Pleas was found, October 1840   PRO 1/4

putrid filth, stench, dirt and decomposition". The records of King's Bench "had to be reached by a ladder and consulted by candle-light where they lay covered with 'soot and filth' in the roof of the Augmentation Office". As Sir Hilary Jenkinson later remarked, the attitude of many departments towards their records was simply "Thou may'st not kill but need'st not strive Officiously to keep alive".

In 1732, as a result of a disastrous fire in the Cottonian Library, a House of Commons Committee was appointed to survey the public records. It identified seventeen different repositories and published a *General Table of the Records of the Kingdom* which showed where each class of record was stored. Government money sponsored publication of the medieval Parliament Rolls and

Domesday Book between 1767 and 1783.

In 1800, a Select Committee was appointed "to inquire into the State of the Public Records" and reported on some 80 different repositories in which the records of central government were kept, as well as local, private and Scottish records, although it did not cover the records of government departments such as the Treasury and the War Office. It reported that "the most essential of all the measures recommended by them for the purpose of laying open to the public a full knowledge of the contents of our various and extensive record repositories, would be unquestionably to print some of the principal calendars and indexes". This led to the appointment of a Record Commission, the first of six which were appointed between 1800 and 1831. These Commissions spent over £400,000 on the publication of record texts such as the Statutes of the Realm and the early Charter, Patent and Close Rolls, but little on the proper storage, arrangement and indexing of the records themselves. They offered no solution to the problem of an ever increasing accumulation scattered throughout so many different repositories.

High fees continued to be a source of complaint. In 1830, the antiquarian Sir Nicholas Harris Nicolas castigated the charges at the Tower Record Office, where "no individual can inspect a document which is confessedly the property of the public, and for the conservation of which the public is taxed, without paying the sum of sixteen shillings and eight pence of which sum ten shillings is for making the search, as it is termed, and six shillings and eight pence for one of the clerks rising from his chair, walking a few yards, and opening a roll .. The expense of a mere transcript of a public record, from a public office, the keeper of which receives £500 per annum from the public .. amounts altogether to very nearly as much as is paid for an original article in a popular publication".

A Proposal for the Erection of a General Record Office

In 1831, the Master of the Rolls, Sir John Leach, proposed that Rolls House, where he no longer lived, and the Rolls Chapel form the nucleus of a central repository. This idea was developed by C R Cooper, Secretary of the Commission, who published in 1832 *A Proposal for the Erection of a General Record Office .. on the site of the Rolls Estate*. There was a pressing need for new accommodation and this had been acknowledged by the Chancellor of the Exchequer who, on a visit to the Tower Record Office in 1823, had pronounced that "a proper building ought to be immediately erected in some more accessible part of the metropolis, capable of uniting and containing all the national Records". Cooper argued that the obvious site for this was the Rolls Estate. It occupied two acres in the very heart of legal London where most professional record users were based. It lay between two Inns of Court, Simonds Inn to the north and Sergeants' Inn to the south, bounded by Chancery Lane to the west and Fetter Lane to the east. As Rolls House was no longer used as a private residence by the Master of the Rolls, it had already been pressed into service for the storage of legal records. By selling or leasing part of the estate to lawyers for chambers, ironically an alternative use suggested for the site in 1995-1996, sufficient revenue could be raised to develop the rest of the site as Record Office and courts. Many speculative builders, it was argued, would take this on and thereby private capital could be injected into public works in a project worthy of the Private Finance Initiative of the 1990s.

Cooper also wanted to extend the existing fee-based system. Instead of the records being scattered in various repositories "most of which are known only to a few "record Agents", unsorted, unarranged, unindexed, and sometimes abandoned to the custody of clerks unable to read a common Latin document", they should be held in one place with "ample Indexes to the whole". With better access, fee income would rise to £6,000 p.a. and this would more than defray the salaries of the keepers and their clerks. He did not elaborate in detail as to how these "ample indexes" were to be created. Presumably not by the existing staff as "no change is propounded with reference to the emoluments, or duties, of the existing Keepers; and an alteration in the mere locality of a sinecure would not, it is hoped, be productive of grave inconvenience". To economise on storage costs, all documents "merely of a historical, or antiquarian, character .. should be transferred to the British Museum".

In 1836, Charles Buller MP moved that a Select Committee of the House of Commons be appointed to

18

enquire into the Record Commission's work and his speech enunciated the guiding principles on which the Public Record Office was to be established. "The first great object was that those records should be kept in a convenient place in security and good arrangement; the next, that there should be proper calendars and indexes; the third, that all records which were in any danger of perishing should be transcribed and, in cases where printing happened to be not too expensive, that such records should be printed." The Select Committee wound up the Record Commission and recommended that the public records be brought together into one general repository and under a single custody. The obvious site was the Rolls Estate and when Lord Langdale was appointed Master of the Rolls in 1836 the government had made it clear that he was to hold the Rolls Estate only as trustee. In the following year it was vested in the Crown by the Rolls Estate Act. This paved the way for the Public Record Office Act of 1838 and the development of the Chancery Lane site into what its first Deputy Keeper, Sir Francis Palgrave called "the strong box of the Empire".

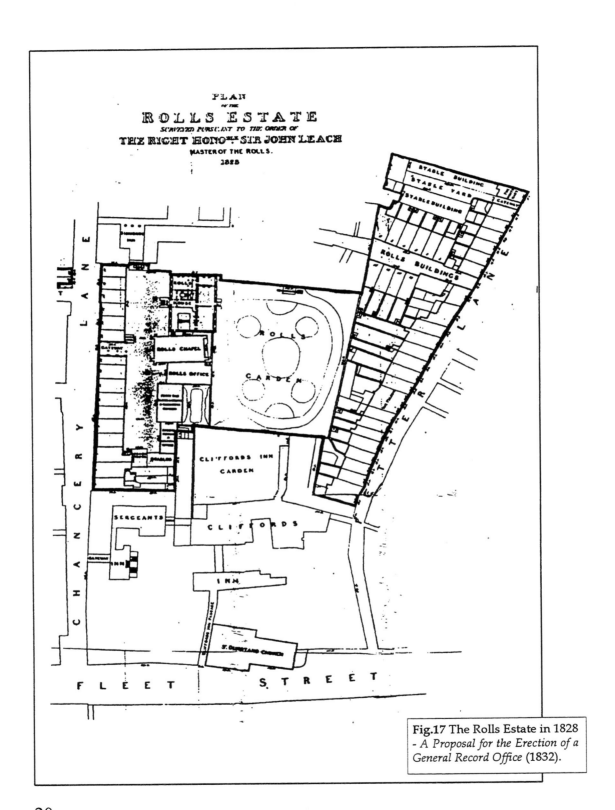

PLAN
of the
ROLLS ESTATE
SURVEYED PURSUANT TO THE ORDER OF
THE RIGHT HONO. Sir JOHN LEACH
MASTER OF THE ROLLS.
1828

Fig.17 The Rolls Estate in 1828
- *A Proposal for the Erection of a
General Record Office* (1832).

Establishment and building of the public record office

The Public Record Office Acts of 1838-1898

n 1838 the Public Record Office was established by the Public Record Office Act. This distinguished between the records of Chancery, which were specifically placed in the custody of the Master of the Rolls, and other "Records belonging to Her Majesty which now are or ought to be deposited in the several Record Offices, Courts, Places and Custody herein-after mentioned", essentially medieval and legal records, which were to be in his "charge and superintendence". Lord Langdale, then Master of the Rolls, took a keen interest in the establishment of the Record Office and this was later commemorated in the naming of one of the reading rooms in the Kew building, the Langdale Room.

The Master of the Rolls was to "have full Power to make such Orders as he may think fit for cleaning, repairing, preserving and arranging all the Public Records under his Charge and Superintendence, and for making Calendars, Catalogues, and Indexes to the same". He was also empowered to appoint a "Chief Record Keeper" as Deputy Keeper and other assistants and to "make Rules for dispensing with the Payment of Fees in such Cases as he shall think fit". The Act required the Treasury to provide "such suitable and proper additional Building or Buildings as may be required".

The Act did not cover the state papers or the records of "modern" government departments. However, once established, certain departments, including the Treasury, saw the convenience of having a central repository for their own non-current records and began to transfer large quantities of records to it. In 1845, the Master of the Rolls defined, in a letter to the Treasury, just what the duties of the Public Record Office were, in respect to these non-statutory deposits:

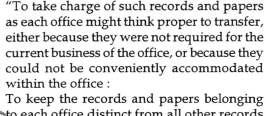

"To take charge of such records and papers as each office might think proper to transfer, either because they were not required for the current business of the office, or because they could not be conveniently accommodated within the office :

To keep the records and papers belonging to each office distinct from all other records and papers :

To arrange them, and cause proper calendars and indexes of them to be made :

To hold them for the special use of the offices to which they respectively belong :

To make searches and transcripts whenever required for the use of Government or Parliament :

To transmit the originals to the office from which they came, if and when required for the use of the office :

And to afford access and inspection to the public or to individuals, only in pursuance of orders given by the head of the office from which they came, or some person authorised by him : or in pursuance of general or special rules approved by him".

Writing in 1949, Sir Hilary Jenkinson, then Deputy Keeper, wrote that "the position of the Record Office .. has continued, in fact, to be down to the present date very much that prescribed for it, by Lord Langdale as an interim measure in 1845". In effect, the Office was acting as an agency for other departments. This position was ratified by Order in Council in 1852 which placed "all records belonging to Her Majesty deposited in any office, court, place or custody" under the charge and superintendence of the Master of the Rolls.

Faced with the Office's demands for ever more accommodation to house these departmental records, the Treasury questioned the wisdom of keeping so much. In 1874, the Financial Secretary to the Treasury, W H Smith, asked "are we not accumulating such a mass of paper and ink and print as to render it impossible for the future student of the Records of these times to make any use of the materials he will find? Will he not be completely overwhelmed with the masses of perfectly valueless matter which he will find?" To limit the transfer of records deemed unworthy of permanent preservation, a further Act of 1877 laid down procedures for the review and destruction of unwanted documents post-dating 1715. Destruction schedules were to be laid before Parliament for 4 weeks before action was taken. In 1882, a permanent committee of inspecting officers', consisting of the Deputy Keeper, an assistant keeper and a barrister, was established to draw up annual schedules, in conjunction with a representative of any department whose records were under discussion. An Act of 1898 required the Office to preserve all records pre-dating 1660, instead of 1715 as formerly.

Staff and Readers

᷂᷂᷂᷂᷂᷂᷂᷂᷂᷂᷂᷂᷂᷂᷂᷂᷂᷂᷂᷂᷂᷂᷂

Sir Francis Palgrave, a barrister and medieval historian who had been a sub-commissioner with the Record Commission, was appointed as the first Deputy Keeper in charge of the new Record Office. Based at Rolls House, he inherited six branch record offices - the Rolls Chapel, Rolls House, the Tower of London Record Office, Carlton Ride (once the indoor riding school of the Prince Regent), the Augmentation Office and the Westminster Chapter House, with a staff of 22 keepers and clerks and 11 workmen for the cleaning, repairing, packing and stamping of records.

In 1840, the workmen petitioned Palgrave for a pay increase arguing that their weekly wage of £1 5s compared badly with rates paid for comparable work at the British Museum and left them with a mere 3½d over after all necessities of existence, including two pints of beer a day, had been deducted. They were turned down. Cheap labour was at a discount and none were in trade unions. At Carlton Ride, the workmen were given a beer allowance of a pint a day as a stimulus to encourage the men engaged on "unwholesome" work. "Beer money" was also paid when records were being moved in bulk to the new Chancery Lane building. When this was completed in 1859, Palgrave issued new regulations forbidding bringing beer into the office other than at lunch time.

PUBLIC RECORD OFFICE.

Regulations as to Workmen.

1 A Workman is not to leave the Public Record Office, between 8 and 4, unless sent by the Deputy - Keeper, Secretary, an Assistant - Keeper, or the Care - Taker; or passed out by the Senior Foreman on duty, for some special reason. Any breach of this Regulation to be reported as speedily as is convenient, to the Secretary.

2 BEER is not to be brought in for the Workmen, except between 12 and 2; and, in the Repository, into the Kitchen (D. 12) only, where all cooking, meals, &c., for the Repository is to take place: - SPIRITS are not to be introduced at any time, except in case of illness with the sanction of an Assistant - Keeper.

3 The Officers of the Service, the Foremen, and the Policemen are requested and empowered to enforce these Regulations, and to report immediately to the Deputy - Keeper or Secretary any infringement thereof, or any case of Drunkenness; *which will be punished by Reduction or Suspension of Wages, Degradation to a lower Class, or Dismissal from the Service.*

(*Signed*) FRANCIS PALGRAVE, D. K.

18 *November*, 1859.

Fig. 18 Regulations as to Workmen, 1859. PRO 8/29 p.285

By early 1841, the number of workmen had more than doubled to 26 and in his *Report* for 1844, Palgrave acknowledged that much of the preliminary sorting of records was done by workmen, some of whom had "such a degree of knowledge as to be able not only to distinguish the age of the more ancient Records, but also the classes to which they belong". From 1862, the editors of the calendars of state papers began to train some of the more promising "in a knowledge of the ancient handwritings, in Latin, Norman-French etc., and in abstracting ancient documents" and these were re-graded as "Transcribers". More clerks were appointed, some employed to make office copies of modern records, typically (in 1860) paid 5d an hour for a 48-hour week. By 1872, the staff consisted of the Deputy Keeper, paid a salary of £1,000 p.a.; 7 First Class Assistant Keepers at £500-£800; 25 clerks on £100-£400; 49 workmen paid £52-£83 4s, with a superintendent on £124 16s, and 5 charwomen who received £26 a year.

After 1894, the workmen of what was then known as "the Subordinate Establishment", which embraced everything from coal heavers to skilled document repairers, were re-organised into Attendants, who worked on the preservation, arrangement and production of records; Messengers, and Porters. For security purposes, the Metropolitan Police assigned four constables to the record service, later increased to 10 constables and a sergeant. A "hall-porter" was appointed in 1881 to exclude from the search rooms "unsavoury and unclean persons".

Palgrave died in post in 1861 and was succeeded by T D Hardy, who was succeeded in 1878 by his brother, William Hardy, under whom it was said the Office "Did nothing in particular. And did it very well". When William Hardy was succeeded by Henry Maxwell Lyte in 1886, the latter was urged by one of the Assistant Keepers, Hubert Hall that "Certain recognised indulgences might be gently discouraged *pro communi salute* e.g. such as are believed to give rise to (surely) needless scandal at the expense of the Service; namely, prolonged conversation (which wastes at a moderate computation one third of the time of half the Office), habitual reading of the newspapers; letter writing; amateur cookery; and all other attempts to convert the Office into a private club".

Fig. 19 Public Entrance to the Reading Rooms, with bust of Lord Langdale.

From 1838, all the offices were open to searchers from 10 a.m. to 4 p.m., every day except for Sundays and public holidays. Fees for consulting the records were reduced by 80% and the number of searches has been estimated to have risen by some 60% over the old system. For so-called "literary inquiries" i.e. historical research, rather than professional use of the records for legal purposes, there was a fee of one shilling a week to consult the finding aids and then another shilling for the consultation of each record. Alternatively there was an all inclusive search fee of five shillings per week for searches limited to one family, place or subject. Palgrave's attitude to charges, expressed in a letter to Lord Langdale in 1839, was that "whilst on the one hand it is unjust to fix so high a rate as to impose an oppressive tax upon those who have occasion to use the Records, or to view the fees as a source of revenue, and therefore to be raised to the highest practicable amount - it is on the other hand equally undesirable to fix them at so low a rate as to encourage idle or unnecessary applications, by which the public time of the officers will be broken up and wasted". In 1851, a petition asking for literary searches to be exempted from fees was forwarded to the Master of the Rolls by the President of the Society of Antiquaries. Signed by luminaries such as Carlyle, Dickens, Hallam and Macaulay, it argued that public documents were "the only sure foundation of historical truth" and that if historians were deterred from using them by heavy fees, they would be "compelled to copy erroneous or questionable statements from earlier authors .. thus doubt and mistake are perpetuated and made part of our national history". Fee income to the public purse was negligible "except to those who pay it. The attainment of historical truth - an object in which the whole nation is interested - is therefore prejudiced, and in many cases defeated by the enforcement of fees which produce the nation absolutely nothing".

New rules were issued in 1852 by the Master of the Rolls, Sir John Romilly. Grateful readers subscribed to a marble bust to their benefactor inscribed "He opened the fount of learning". One of the Kew reading rooms was later to be named the Romilly Room in his memory. These rules allowed the Deputy Keeper to allow those working for literary purposes to consult both indexes and original records without charge and to make copies or extracts from them in pencil. It was clearly stated that "it will not be possible for the Officers to assist any literary inquirers beyond the production of the documents and giving a general explanation, if needed, of their character and nature. No applicant ought to present himself who is not sufficiently acquainted with the handwriting, abbreviations and language of ancient documents,". Access conditions were set by transferring departments: the Treasury and War Office allowed access to post-1820 records but for the Home Office the closure date was 1760 and for the Foreign Office, 1688.

Fig. 20 Bust of Lord Romilly

At first, no more than 30 places were provided for searchers in the new Chancery Lane building. In the 1850s this was probably more than sufficient. Between 1852 and 1860 there were only 939 literary enquirers making 11,609 visits. Even by the 1890s there were no more than 40-50 readers a day. Nonetheless, strongrooms were reorganised so that records most in demand were placed nearest to the search rooms. The rule that readers should not be allowed to order up more than three records at a time was introduced in 1866.

Deputy Keeper A E Stamp later recalled that in 1891 "there was not a typed list or typewriter in the office .. the only way for a stranger to find out anything in the records [of the War Office and Admiralty] was to explain what he wanted and trust to the staff to produce it. For officers of the department there was a back room in which sat an ancient attendant surrounded by MS. War Office lists in all stages of decay and illegibility. Tradition said that he knew his way about them, but few dared to approach him, and those who did were as a rule only rewarded with a supercilious stare over ancient *pince-nez*, and the answer that the question propounded was a difficult one and required mature consideration. So far as my own experience went, it seldom received it". Dust was then a major problem, until the introduction of a vacuum cleaner, and every document asked for had to be cleaned with a duster before it could be used. In the search rooms, "there used to be great competition for places near the fires on cold days, and corresponding avoidance when the weather was warmer". Stamp also recalled "a certain number of elderly gentlemen who seemed to have been driven to the Public Record Office by lack of sleeping accommodation in the reading-room of the British Museum. Whatever their self-imposed business may have been, they used to come day after day and sleep away the office hours".

In 1875, one disgruntled regular reader, John Pym Yeatman, published *An Exposure of the Mismanagement of the Public Record Office*, accusing its officials of "hereditary corruption" and describing the external clerical editors it employed as "vampires upon the establishment". He drew a sharp contrast with the "comfort and convenience" of the British Museum and condemned the "enormous salaries" of the Assistant Keepers when compared with the meagre wages of the workmen grades who "are only kept from getting up a strike under terror of instant dismissal". Indexes to the records were poor and readers had to wait too long for documents. In 1876, he took the Office to court to force it to allow him to inspect certain documents to which he had been refused access. The Court of Appeal ultimately ruled that there was "no general right in all the Queen's subjects to inspect the documents in the Record Office". He was still launching complaints in 1899.

All admission fees were abolished in 1866 but in 1887 fees were re-introduced for legal documents post 1760 to discourage "unnecessary applications" and the Treasury then also introduced a fee of 1s per document for those consulting its post-1759 documents. Its Permanent Secretary wrote to the Deputy Keeper in 1889, "I cannot see what justification there is for expensive staff being kept for the benefit of private individuals, often foreigners, who amuse themselves or seek their bread in literary pursuits". Originally cards of admission were introduced for such literary searchers but this had lapsed by 1866 when all that was required was to sign in the attendance register.

The Building of the Public Record Office

The Treasury had originally proposed to house the public records in the Victoria Tower of the newly built Houses of Parliament, as the most economical solution to providing a central record repository, but it soon became clear that this would never provide sufficient space. An alternative site proposed was Westminster Prison. Westminster was held to be damp and ill-drained whereas the Rolls Estate was high above the river and on gravel soil.

In 1850, Parliament voted £30,000 towards the estimated total cost of £45,320 for building a new repository on the Rolls Estate site although the central block alone was ultimately to cost twice this (£88,490). The foundation stone of the "treasure house of the Public Records or Archives" was laid on the Queen's Birthday, 24 May 1851 and the records were moved in 1856. The architect was James Pennethorne, a pupil of John Nash and then Surveyor of Buildings to the Office of Works. His original designs involved extending Carey St. into a major new road, linking Long Acre and Cheapside, to front the new building, a three-storied Gothic structure, to the north. It had large search rooms, 60 feet long and two floors high and a large decagonal library. For Palgrave, this was too ambitious - "even at 100 years hence Mr Pennethorne's plan would leave about 1,000,000 cubic feet unoccupied". He insisted that there should be "nothing for display, nothing for the attractions of the public", just what was absolutely necessary "for the transaction of work and business at the smallest possible expense".

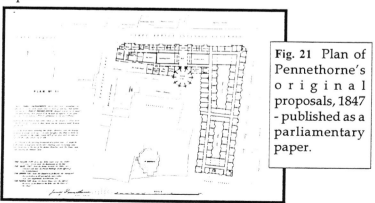

Fig. 21 Plan of Pennethorne's original proposals, 1847 - published as a parliamentary paper.

The result was a building that has been called by Geoffrey Tyack, author of *Sir James Pennethorne and the Making of Victorian London* (Cambridge University Press, 1992) "a rigidly symmetrical building with a tower, of vaguely north-European character, inputting a note of nightmarish fantasy .. The sheer heaviness of the unrelieved elevations, with the monotonous repetition of a single motif - three superimposed windows set within a pointed relieving arch resting on buttresses (a motif found in the fourteenth-century Papal palace at Avignon) is very intimidating, as it was presumably intended to be." It was, nonetheless, "one of the most forward-looking buildings of its age" in the determination of form by function, with the "overpowering massiveness" of Victorian prisons, workhouses and hospitals, an effect enhanced by the user of Kentish rag stone to face the building. Contemporaries were less enthusiastic. One critic described its style as "misapplied and distorted" Tudor. Another spoke of the "strong and dark" repository as "a congeries of caves too confined for the purpose".

Fig. 22 Foundation stone of the Public Record Office.

The burning of the Houses of Parliament in 1834, according to popular legend caused by the incineration of defunct tally sticks (notched sticks used to record accounts), made security from fire the primary consideration in design. On the advice of James Braidwood, superintendent of the London Fire Brigade, the repository area was divided up into small self-contained fire-proof strong rooms with iron doors. Each was to be 25 feet deep and 15 feet 6 inches high, divided into two equal parts by a floor with gratings. As there was no artificial lighting, large windows were essential - small thick panes of glass in cast-iron frames were used. Each floor rested on wrought iron beams and girders, protected from fire by rows of brick arches, an arrangement commonly found in Victorian warehouses. Irish slate from Valentia Island was imported to minimise further any risk of fire from wooden shelving and all the fixtures were to be iron. Pennethorne guaranteed that "no conflagration could ever break out in a fire-proof Record Room".

For additional security, all the presses in which records were stored were fitted with locked wire doors so that when a repository assistant fetched one document, he would only have access to one press in each room. It was even argued that "no Workman should enter a Record Room, except accompanied by a Superior Officer". The wire doors proved so impractical, requiring 4,000 keys for the whole building, that they had to be removed in 1859. The top and first floors of the new building, A and B floors, were intended for record storage, with search rooms on the ground floor (C floor) and stores and accommodation for "papers of secondary importance" in the basement (D floor).

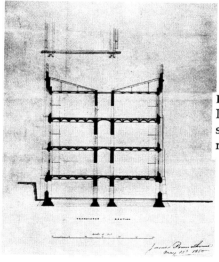

Fig. 23
Pennethorne's section of the repository floor.

Fig.24 Alan Jensen and Bill Goldup inspect slate shelves removed from strongrooms that were later converted to other purposes. Note the prefabricated huts of 1946, used by the Conservation Department, on the right.

The main entrance was by a Gothic doorway in the centre of the south front, to which access was gained via Fetter Lane. This remained the case until after the Second World War. Until then it was far more common for the Office to be known colloquially as "Fetter Lane" rather than as "Chancery Lane". Over this entrance was a tower, originally only constructed to parapet level, not the clock-tower rival to "Big Ben" that appears in Pennethorne's original design. It was completed in 1867 and decorated with statutes of four queens, Victoria, Anne, Elizabeth and Matilda, all carved by Joseph Durham; coats of arms of England, Wales, Scotland and Ireland; of Langdale and Romilly and of various kings and queens. It eventually housed a large water tank to douse any fires that might arise.

Fig.25 Details from the Tower - gargoyles were supplied by the sculptor at 20s. apiece.

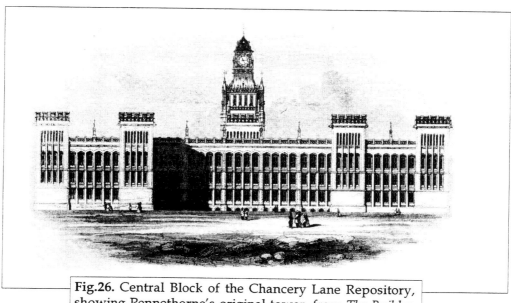

Fig.26. Central Block of the Chancery Lane Repository, showing Pennethorne's original tower, from *The Builder*, 1851.

Until electric lighting was introduced in 1889, there was no artificial lighting in the search rooms which effectively had to close at dusk. According to office tradition, staff "played out time" with a hand of piquet in the corridors by the light of a storm lantern. Colza oil lanterns (paraffin was too dangerous) had to be used in the strongrooms and anecdotes are told of the repository assistant who had to regularly climb "a ladder .. with a lantern held between his teeth" to get down bundles of Chancery Proceedings from strongrooms on D floor. Heating was not originally required either, for staff or documents, Palgrave's view being that "warming effected by the contrivance of flues, pipes and the like, is positively injurious to the health of those employed". Thick walls helped to maintain a reasonably equable temperature but this could be decidedly chilly. Eventually it proved necessary to install glass doors in the corridor "to mitigate the arctic cold of the Repository". Flues in the repositories encouraged air circulation and allowed for the possibility of conversion into offices. Open fire-places were later put into certain offices and the Round reading room.

Listing and Publication

Once the new building was erected and records had been transferred into its strongrooms, priority was given to publication, rather than the arrangement, listing and indexing of those records. Lists and indexes were published as appendices in the Annual Reports of the Deputy Keeper which became so bulky that the Stationery Office protested at the costs of printing them.

In his *Seventeenth Report*, published in 1855, Deputy Keeper Palgrave argued that an ambitious publication programme was a "national duty" and that it was vital to extend facilities for home study as "a quiet hour spent by a student at his own desk with his own tools, is worth a day in any public library". He argued that publication was "a constant instigation to diligence of the Officers employed thereon .. the means of encouraging competition without awakening jealousy or rivalry". To accelerate the production of the calendars of state papers that the State Paper Office had started, he began to employ outside editors, paid according to the number of sheets printed (£8 8s for each sheet of 16 pages), to work on detailed calendars of the state papers. Mrs Mary Everett Green, the most prolific of these editors, produced 41 volumes between 1855 and 1895, the year of her death. The most ambitious of these publications was *Letters and Papers, Foreign and Domestic, of the reign of Henry VIII,*

34

edited by J S Brewer who is said, when sorting documents, to have simply created four piles - 'Henry VIII', 'Not Henry VIII', 'Trash' and 'Rubbish'.

Another great editorial project, sponsored by the Master of the Rolls, and therefore known as the "Rolls Series", *Chronicles and Memorials of Great Britain and Ireland during the Middle Ages*, produced over 250 volumes, of variable quality, only twenty of which were, in the main, Public Record Office material, between 1858 and 1897. Very much the brain-child of Palgrave's successor, T D Hardy, it was paid for by the Treasury which observed in 1866 that "it cannot be expected that works of this kind should meet with a prompt sale or find their way into the hands of the general reader" but that they were "materials placed in store for the advantage of students of history in all time to come".

The period 1856-1886 saw what R B Wernham, himself an editor of state papers foreign for many years, has called "a riot of publishing", which went beyond the main series of state papers, Domestic, Foreign, Irish and Colonial, to embrace material in the foreign archives of Spain, Paris, Venice, Milan and Rome, described in ever fuller calendar summaries. According to Wernham "this energetic attention to partially irrelevant publications .. gravely hindered the work both of developing efficient methods of record preservation and of sorting, arranging and listing - in fact, of making accessible - the public records themselves".

The balance was redressed after Henry Maxwell Lyte took over as Deputy Keeper in 1886, remaining in office until 1926. In this period, the Office concentrated on publishing the records in its custody and the Rolls Series was discontinued. New calendars of medieval records - Patent, Close, Charter and Fine Rolls; Feudal Aids and Inquisitions Post Mortem - were undertaken by members of staff working to a very high standard. Calendars of Treasury Books and Papers were also published, one editor, W A Shaw, producing forty volumes between 1897 and 1939. In 1922, the Office also began to publish texts of early *Curia Regis* rolls. Publications such as these established an academic tradition within the Office and academic reputation outside it, creating what John Cantwell has called "its peculiar mystique as a part-governmental, part-scholarly institution". From the early

1890s, the *Lists and Indexes* series published summary lists of whole record classes, some merely giving the covering dates of each item or piece. According to Maxwell Lyte, this series "combined with the series of calendars issued in royal octavo will eventually constitute a general catalogue of the contents of the Public Record Office while the calendars published in imperial 800, will continue to give abstracts so full as in most cases to supersede the necessity of consulting the original manuscripts. The Lists and Indexes will serve as guides to those who desire to work in the Public Search Room."

Principles of archival arrangement had been infrequently considered in previous surveys of the public records. In 1719, Mr Anstis, Garter King of Arms, had proposed to the House of Lords Committee that for records of the Courts of Wards and of Requests "each instrument should be reduced according to the Order of Time, with regard to the Subject Matter of it, and the Contents put into Calendars with Three Indexes; One of sirnames, the other of Lands and the Third of Matters, all Alphabetically disposed under the particular counties". Giving evidence to the Commons Select Committee of 1836, Henry Cole, Assistant Keeper at Carlton Ride and future founder of the Victoria and Albert Museum, stated that "the advantage of one mode of arrangement over another cannot be estimated unless the nature of the records is practically known, and the records themselves examined. For some records a topographical arrangement is most suitable, for others a chronological, for others a union of both, and for a fourth an arrangement according to species or classes, and in a fifth an artificial mode is only that which can be adopted."

By the end of the nineteenth century, arrangement by creating department had become the norm, although a number of artificial Special Collections were formed e.g. of manorial court rolls, later to be criticised by the 1910 Royal Commission on the Public Records. One of the Assistant Keepers, Harley Rodney, then in charge of the floors, introduced alpha-numeric document references in the early twentieth century, replacing the long descriptive references that readers previously had to transcribe in full on to paper tickets. As new lists replaced old, even members of staff might be flummoxed. A E Stamp recalled that "records on the shelves were not always called by the same name as in the corresponding list. One sometimes sent out a ticket with a description quite correct according to a current list, only to receive it back after what seemed an infinite wait marked "Not known by this reference." We juniors sometimes knew that this was by way of being a practical joke on the part of some floor attendant, who knew perfectly well what we really wanted; but often we had no means of redress except to get the ticket counter-signed by Mr Scargill-Bird who was known to stand no nonsense".

The first but very incomplete, *Handbook to the Public Records* was published by F S Thomas in 1853. It was replaced in 1891 by S R Scargill-Bird's *Guide* which was also subject based in its approach and revised in 1896 and 1908. Not until 1923-24 was it replaced by M S Giuseppi's *Guide,* which reflected the arrangement of the records by their creating bodies. Giuseppi became the standard work and a new edition was published in the 1960s, parts of which have not yet been superseded.

Extension of the Public Record Office 1856-1900

As early as 1856, the Master of the Rolls was pressing the Treasury to fund the building of a second block on the Chancery Lane site, largely because of an unexpected influx of records from government departments which were temporarily being stored in houses fronting Chancery Lane. The Treasury response was that many documents in the Record Office were "of no value, either in an official, statistical or historical point of view" and it established a Committee on Government Documents to investigate how many of these documents could be destroyed. Beginning its review of War Office documents in 1859, by the end of that year it had sent forty tons of records for pulping. Of 400 tons of Admiralty documents reviewed, 165 tons were destroyed. This only offered a short-term solution to a problem that became insurmountable after the State Paper Office was demolished in 1862 and its records were transferred to Chancery Lane. The small literary searchroom at Chancery Lane, no more than 25 feet by 16, could not cope with the influx of ex-State Paper Office readers. One anonymous reader wrote to *The Times* on 11 March 1862 complaining bitterly of "that dismal prison house, like the solitary wing of a lunatic asylum, to which the prudence of the Government and the artistic grace of Mr Pennethorne have consigned the materials of our English History from the Norman Conquest to this year of grace. Piled up the walls from basement to coping, thrust into every sort of nook and corner, stored away and battened down in inconceivable galleries and hatchways, bursting out of crevices, making ghostly appearances at dim windows, like an overcharged warehouse, the present repository stands brimful, ready to spill over with the least addition". He was especially critical of the reading room where, once one had deducted the space occupied by members of staff, he claimed only 10 square feet remained for readers and "I feel in my own single person quite competent to fill an area of 10ft when I am engaged in any pursuit involving some research".

Fig.27 Round Reading Room, c.1925

Work on the extension began in 1863 and was completed in 1868. Two new reading rooms were added: the Legal Search Room, later known as the Long Room, 60 feet long and 26 feet wide, backing on to Fetter Lane and a dodecagonal Literary Search Room, later known as the Round Room, top-lit by a glass dome 44 feet 9 inches in diameter and 46 feet high. It had two storeys and a gallery and was not unlike Smirke's Round Reading Room at the British Museum. Geoffrey Tyack compares its use of structural ironwork to the now demolished Coal Exchange and describes it as "one of the finest remaining examples of Victorian cast-iron architecture in London". A Government Search Room was sited in the middle of the building for readers who had permission to see documents not generally open to the public. Another block was added 1869-1871 at the Fetter Lane end. Tudor style ogee-shaped turrets were introduced which dominated the sky-line and were copied on the later Chancery Lane front, to give the building one of its most characteristic features.

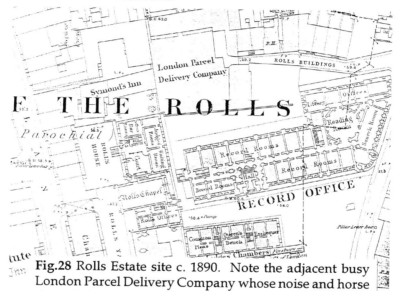

Fig.28 Rolls Estate site c. 1890. Note the adjacent busy London Parcel Delivery Company whose noise and horse dung disturbed users of the Long Room for many years.

By 1889, the Deputy Keeper was pressing for the demolition of the houses fronting Chancery Lane with their 'bulging walls and deciduous chimneys', which had been pressed into service for records storage, and the building of an extension to replace them. Sir John Taylor, Pennethorne's official successor, designed a new frontage on Chancery Lane which became known as 'H Block'. Built between 1892 and 1896 of the more durable Babbacombe limestone, rather than Kentish rag, it housed offices and a library, as well as strongrooms. The new gateway had statues of Henry III, founder of the House of Converts, and Edward III, who united the offices of

Keeper of the Rolls of Chancery with Keeper of the House of Converts. To link it to the existing block, Rolls House and the Rolls Chapel had to be demolished. In 1899, the Judges' Chambers on the south side of the building were demolished and replaced by a garden. The Record Commission of 1914 recommended a further extension to the office along this southern line which had been Pennethorne's original intention, and building on the garden was again considered in the 1960s, when it elicited a curious novel about the Chancery Lane site - Evelyn Berckmann's *The Blessed Plot* (Hamish Hamilton, 1976). Instead, a new building was erected at Kew which opened in 1977. Geoffrey Tyack compares it to Pennethorne's structure as a monument of severe functionalism.

Fig.29 Chancery Lane Front, 1895.

By the end of the nineteenth century, the Norwich antiquarian Walter Rye was contrasting the inconveniences of the Long Room in the 1870s "a long unpleasant room, with low tables and high backless forms, which cramped the searcher's legs if he were anything above a dwarf" with a present situation in which "it would be difficult to find a place where study and search can be carried on more easily and pleasantly .. certainly at no place are the officials, from the highest to the lowest, more courteous or more willing to help. The beginner, stumbling along, and only half conscious as to what he is looking for, is as well treated and listened to as patiently as the *habitué*; and with the single exception of lunatics, who want information about unclaimed millions "in Chancery", who are sternly kept at bay by a standing notice in the lobby, all searchers, however different their objects, are made welcome". This was because "there is hardly a clerk in the office who does not take an active and intelligent interest in some class of records, and who has not contributed something to their history". His only wish was that the hours be extended into the evenings, now that the electric light made this possible, and that the "barbaric rule" banning the use of ink pens be rescinded. In his *Records and Record Searching*, he recommended the names of competent record agents for those unable to carry out searches themselves.

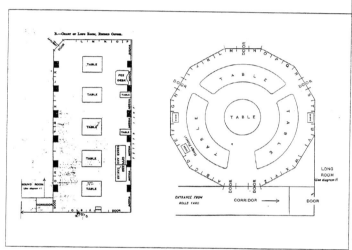

Fig.30 Plans of the Round Room and the Long Room from William Rye's *Records and Record Searching* (1897). A E Stamp was later to say of the Long Room arrangement that it was "calculated to give every one except the officer at the desk the minimum of natural light on their work, while giving the officer the maximum of draught on his back".

Consolidation and war, 1900-1958

Royal Commission on the Public Records

n 1910, following agitation by Welsh nationalists to have Welsh records in the Public Record Office transferred to Wales, bolstered by criticism made by historians that they were not involved in the selection of documents for permanent preservation and against the retention of records by departments, a Royal Commission on the Public Records was appointed. It published three reports between 1912 and 1919, the appendices of which are a vital source for the early history of the Office. The Commission made many recommendations, from limited expansion on the Chancery Lane site to the building of a new office next to the proposed Imperial War Museum to house twentieth-century departmental records. The report called for regular transfer of departmental records and opening up more record classes to public inspection, stating that "no useful purpose can be served by the suppression of historical facts or the concealment of documentary evidence except in the case of matters so recent as to be confidential". Use of book-rests in the search rooms should be made compulsory. It also recommended that properly trained staff should be appointed to the record sections of each government department which should be run by the PRO as branches of its main operation and that local record offices should also be brought under the superintendence of the Master of the Rolls. Against the background of the Great War, these recommendations had little impact.

Fig.31 Assistant keeper C G Crump and Professor Tout outside the Record Office.

42

Listing and Publication

Evidence submitted to the Royal Commission criticised the Office's creation of "Special Collections", rather than leaving them in an arrangement by creating department. William Page, General Editor of the Victoria County History, gave evidence that "of late years there has been a tendency at the Record Office to group together documents of a similar nature like Ministers' Accounts, Rentals, Surveys and so on. This is an immense convenience to ordinary searchers, but you to a certain extent lose a part of the history". Professor Tout stated that "it would be unwise to break up the ancient *fonds* [collections]; they are inconvenient, but on the whole it is best to keep them as they have been handed down to us". Professor Little felt that "the Record Office has been doing almost too much for the public in the way of having too much regard for the immediate interests of searchers, and too little for the records themselves as the results of the administrative machinery".

The Office had already addressed this problem. One of the assistant keepers, Harley Rodney, stated: "I do not think it would be a good thing for us to mess records about. There is a danger of destroying historical evidence; a record is a thing that should grow up in its natural state and remain as it is made. Directly we begin undoing things, we destroy the evidence as to how they were done, but we cannot always help doing it". The Office ceased to create new special collections and the future arrangement of records was dictated by principles of archival provenance, the key textbook for which was to be written by Hilary Jenkinson, a future Deputy Keeper.

The period 1900-1958 saw the beginnings of a shift away from publications and towards arrangement and listing as the main focus of curatorial activity. Much pioneering work was done by Harley Rodney, who had joined the Office as a clerk in 1879, rising to senior clerk in 1893 and assistant keeper in 1906. His *Times* obituary in 1930 read: "His chief official work, by which he will always be remembered, was his reduction to some sort of order of the flotsam and jetsam which had accumulated during many centuries. He had the proper combination of qualities for the task, a sense of proportion, an unwearied patience and energy, and an ability to take long views; he never asked any man working under him to undertake any task in which he was not himself prepared to share, even though, from a physical point of view, it was severe. The problem he was set to solve did not allow him to consider fine points of provenance, though he had the necessary scholarship; in fact, any appreciable progress in arranging the accumulation of many years was quite inconsistent with detailed examination of individual documents." Described as "a man's man", Rodney also wrote a number of novels including *Hilda - A Study in Passion*, *A Treble Soloist* and *Gummy's Island*, copies of which are in the Office Library.

Fig.32 Harley Rodney as a sergeant of Special Constables c. 1916. PRO 8/55.

The priorities identified by Jenkinson were "first, methodical and complete Sorting, Numeration and Listing: second, a simple System of Reference equally applicable to Records of any class, date, shape or form .. third, a Directory to the Contents of the Office in a form which can never become obsolete and is capable of indefinite expansion: and finally, a corollary to these, a settled system for the physical Arrangement of the Records in the Repository". He acknowledged that errors had occurred in the past, breaking up series whose form had changed or bringing together artificial collections covering the same subject, but pointed out that "knowledge of the right way has come through one generation doing wrong and another observing the results". Class lists i.e. "a setting down of all the Numbers in a Class in order and adding to each the barest detail necessary to identify the piece - very generally, its date" were essentially "an instrument for the Repository staff". Not until 1912 was a complete summary list of records made available in the search rooms and this, Jenkinson records, was regarded as "a revolutionary proceeding".

The Royal Commission did not think that "the two functions of preserving the archives of the nation and publishing them should be permanently combined .. they were not intended to be combined when the Public Record Office was established and they are not so combined in other countries". Nevertheless both functions continued as before, with publications still dominated by medieval series. In 1947, the Office established a Consultative Committee which included representatives from universities to advise on the future direction of Office publications. In view of the ever increasing bulk of records, it became clear that printed publications could not provide a final solution to "remote access", "the problem of the 'Student at a distance,". Jenkinson argued that selections were not appropriate as "the Department, taking a long view, must provide not only for immediate but for possible future interests" and so must aim for comprehensive coverage. Medieval documents should have priority because of their rarity - a curious argument from one who always emphasised the uniqueness of every document, whether medieval or modern. His view was that photographic reproduction and easier travel made the production of calendars less important than descriptive lists which would allow the remote user to decide what was worth copying. Jenkinson suggested these lists be published in microform. He also argued that more editors be employed as "while it is considered essential that all members of staff in the higher grades should be engaged to some considerable extent in 'editorial' work .. the volume of administrative work is too great to .. produce so large an output as is desired".

Staff and Readers

By 1908, there were 105 members of staff of whom 37 were curatorial and administrative staff and 68 "support" staff i.e. repository assistants, messengers, porters, conservation craftsmen etc. Over the period 1882 to 1936, the number of assistant keeper or equivalent posts fell

by 34%. There was little change in the overall number of staff in the inter-war period but this had risen to 158 by 1948 and by 1951 the Office was authorised to have 177 staff. When this figure was cut back to 154 by the Treasury, Deputy Keeper Jenkinson reacted by closing the Office Museum and the smallest of the reading rooms - the South Room. The Treasury subsequently acknowledged the heavy new burdens on the Office due to "the vast increase in paper which seems to flow from modern methods of government .. categories of record which, previous to the war, were not thought to be in the Public Record

Fig.33 "A Fair American looking at Domesday Book" c.1910.

Office phase of life at all" and increased the authorised establishment to 164. By 1958, there were 177 staff in post.

Assistant keepers were recruited through the general Civil Service administrative class examination system until 1929, when a competition specifically for curatorial grades was introduced. There were two grades - AK (I) and AK (II). Roger Ellis, who joined the Office as an assistant keeper in 1934, was later to speak of the way in which "the majesty of the Records themselves fired my imagination from the start. There they lay in their silent caves, great stalactites of history, some left complete, some truncated, as the imperceptible currents of life had turned to run elsewhere, some year by year still growing". On his first day he was told by his training officer, S C Ratcliff, "The first thing to remember about this place, gentlemen, is this: that there is any amount of work to be done, and no hurry whatever about doing it. Here, accuracy is more important than speed". Continuity stood for much. Ellis met the then retired Sir Henry Maxwell Lyte whose own career in the Office had overlapped with members of staff who had been there since its foundation in 1838. An anecdote from another

source relates that on one occasion, Ratcliff is said to have found one of his staff asleep on duty and tiptoed out of the room to avoid waking him. Of one assistant keeper: "F Slingsby passed high in the Civil Service exam and was sent to the Treasury. After a 'good' First World War, in which he won the MC, he began to suffer from narcolepsy (an inability to stay awake), and was promptly transferred to the PRO ... He tended to spend most of his day asleep at his desk, waking in the late afternoon and then working furiously and effectively for an hour or two".

Fig.34 Montague Spencer Giuseppi, assistant keeper 1891-1934. PRO 8/55.

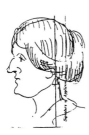

There was a very clear social divide between the assistant keepers and the other staff. Although little different from the 'caste' system that then operated throughout the civil service it survived for many years and even within each level there were distinctions. One assistant keeper, who committed suicide in 1937, came from a state school, unlike most of his public school educated colleagues. It is said that when it was announced that he had thrown himself under a train, one remarked 'He has let the office down again. It wasn't even a main line!' Nonetheless, one member of staff who had joined the PRO as a boy clerk in 1913 "burst through the glass ceiling" to be appointed an assistant keeper in 1937. One recalls "The public-school ethos was alive and kicking well into the 1960s - Z, for example, was a notorious snob about people's social origins; Hector - one of the most astute and learned archivists ever to work at the PRO - was made conscious, all his career, of 'only' being educated at Bristol Grammar School; and H C Johnson, even when Keeper, was permanently at odds with Y and other socially superior types. And I can remember one assistant

keeper, of my own generation, referring to a distinguished university historian who had once been a teacher in a public school as 'only a damned usher,''. He also recalls that "the late Kenneth Timings said of one meritocrat (a brisk administrator with a first in Greats from Oxford), 'until X was appointed, assistant keepers had always been either scholars or gentlemen'" and, speaking of the "sometimes socially divided and administratively lackadaisical zeitgeist of past generations", supplied two further anecdotes -

"At least two members of the PRO's editorial staff ... were left so much to their own devices that no one knew what they were doing, and their editorial work was thrown away when they left the Office".

"There were until (relatively) recently strict rules about accommodation in respect of grading. Clerical staff (AOs or whatever) were not entitled to carpets on the floor, but the rule was relaxed for one particularly clumsy and noisy CO in H20 because the scraping of his chair on the floor annoyed the Keeper in the room below. At one time, there were several spare desks in that room, but a CO was made to work at the communal table in the middle on the grounds that COs were not entitled to individual desks".

Some assistant keepers saw themselves as professional archivists, others as essentially administrative civil servants who just happened to have been posted to the Record Office. Many of those recruited in the 1940s and 1950s were medievalists who ultimately found university teaching posts more congenial. Vivian Galbraith, subsequently Regius Professor at Oxford, saw his assistant keepership as a 'stick-in-the-mud' job but doubted if he would ever find nicer mud to stick in.

Fig.35 Group of assistant keepers in 1955. Deputy Keeper Sir David Evans is in the centre, flanked by Miss Daphne Gifford (l.) and Miss P M Barnes (r.) - PRO 8/74.

THE O.C. L.S.R. BELEIVES IN GETTING THINGS DONE

In 1920, Hilary Jenkinson, who was to become one of the most influential exponents of archival theory in the world and who subsequently became Deputy Keeper in 1947, was promoted to assistant keeper. He reorganised the Round Room so that reference works were classified by the records to which they referred, an arrangement that became familiar to generations of readers and survived little changed up to 1996. Aware that the first thing new readers often asked for (and still do) was a "General Index to the Records" he calculated that in 1949, there were over 30 million documents in the Office and that if an indexer could be employed to index them at a rate of 50 a day, the task would take 3,000 years.

Fig.36 Hilary Jenkinson - PRO 8/53

There was a general reorganisation of clerical staff after the First World War when general Civil Service grades were brought in and again in 1946 when general Civil Service Executive grades were introduced. By 1949, there were 50 posts in the so-called "Higher Establishment" i.e. the Deputy Keeper, one Principal Assistant Keeper, 5 Assistant Keepers directing sections (Secretariat; Repository and Repairs; Search Rooms; Editorial and Training and Museum, Public Relations and 'Guide'); 16 Assistant Keepers; 1 Senior Executive Officer; 3 Higher Executive Officers; 11 Executive Officers and 13 clerks and typists. In the "Subordinate Establishment" was 1 Superintendent; 1 Superintendent of Binding and Repairs; 1 Chief Repairer; 4 Foremen; 6 Sub-Foremen; 16 Class I Attendants and Repairers; 24 Class II Attendants; 12 Attendants; 7 Senior Messengers; 33 Porter-Messengers; 1 Ladies' Attendant and 8 part-time cleaners. There was in the words of one member of staff, a "gulf" between the "minor" grades and the administrative grades to the extent that one attendant was even disciplined for consorting with a clerical officer and told not to wait for her outside the Office after work.

Miss F. learn that they require stamping

After the First World War, some of the old disciplines started to break down. In 1927, the newly established

49

Attendants' and Repairers Association had taken the PRO to an Industrial Court with a significant pay claim. There were then 9 attendants who worked in the search rooms, 12 on document production and 22 repairers.

Fig.37 "The Great Record Office Strike". It is uncertain whether this refers to the industrial dispute of 1927. The figure on the right has been identified as J R Crompton, assistant keeper. PRO 8/53.

Some clerical officers had very long careers with the Office. O G R Fox who joined in 1911, and eventually became Establishment Officer, did not retire until 1960.

Fig.38 O G R Fox c. 1912. PRO 8/55

One repairer recalls that when the Belsize Park repository (see below) was opened, the attendants were ordered to go there to unpack documents. No excess travel fares were then paid and when they refused, Fox "immediately came down and sacked the lot of us". Half an hour later, he repented and established a rota that only required one to go.

Administrative functions became increasingly important as the number of records housed multiplied. Writing in 1949, Jenkinson commented that it would "surprise those who think of the Department simply as an Office where Research is carried out" to learn that "a considerable proportion of the higher staff (4 out of 22 Assistant

Keepers and 5 out of 26 Executive and Clerical Officers) is engaged almost exclusively in the mere organisation of such matters as Shifting and Packing, maintenance of the *Summary*, the Cleaning of the Records, their Make-up and Labelling, the Cleaning and Painting of the Building, the Production of Records to Staff and Public, Weekly Inspections, 'Stock-taking', Fire Precautions, Damp Precautions and Key Control". The attitude of mind expressed by use of the word 'mere' persisted until relatively modern times. The vital role these functions play is now more clearly acknowledged. Significantly, the new inspecting officers appointed to oversee the selection and transfer of records as recommended by the Grigg Report (see below) were appointed to senior executive rather than curatorial grades, although the Records Administration Division to which they were attached was headed by a senior assistant keeper. As John Cantwell comments "a small minority of the older assistant keepers found difficulty in coming to terms with the advance of those they saw as 'jumped-up boy clerks', but the sensible majority accepted the changing order with good grace".

For many years there was also a cat on the establishment, with an official Treasury allowance for its maintenance. It was needed to keep down rats, long a hazard to documents. For many years the skeleton of a rat, preserved with the Exchequer documents, was on display in the Office Museum. Some conservators still on the staff recall the rats at Chancery Lane and their taste for flour paste glue and new repair parchment.

Fig.39 Security guard with Tiger 'the King's Cat', 1915.

Fig.40 Daring theft of a 'De Banco'(CP 40 Plea Roll) - the security guard on duty appears to be the same as that with the cat.

Fig.41 Staff Christmas Party in the Committee Room in 1939. Deputy Keeper Sir Cyril Flower is at the far end of the central table.

Not all was conflict however, the PRO Staff Association organised excursions and dinners at which toasts were launched for the "Officers". The centenary of the Office in 1938 was marked by a Grand Reception at Chancery Lane with over a thousand guests and the band of the Welsh Guards playing in the Round Room.

Fig.42 1913 Dinner Programme.

In 1925, A E Stamp, then the Office's Secretary, defined the policy on postal enquiries. "We have a printed form which says that this department does not undertake searches for the public; but we administer the rule rather easily. If anyone asks if a certain document is in the office we try to say yes or no .. If the demand is for information about a person or subject and we can give an answer without more than a few minutes searching .. we make a search .. Otherwise we offer to supply the names of capable record agents". By the 1930s, there were 80-100 readers a day, many from abroad. Production of documents in the Round Room averaged 55,000-60,000

Fig.43 The Long Room.

a year and in the Long Room, 25,000-30,000. As John Cantwell observes of this period, the office "had never been publicity-conscious and had no wish to make its services better known". A L Rowse, in an article published in *The Spectator* in November 1937 said of his fellow search room users "we all know we are slightly mad".

Hans Breitmann in der Legalroom
He write der Billets op;
Miss Eliot she com to him,
Der Breitmann, he no shtop.
"Oh please, it says here on dese Rolls
Dere are joost ony four
Oh will you say, please, does it mean
Dere are not any more?"

—

Und shtill he write der Billets op
Und answer not a Vurd,
But, ven Miss Eliot shpeak again,
An ask him, if he heard.

He shpat ein shpit wohl on der floor
For all der Welt to see,
Und "Breitmann does not shpeak mit fools"
Said Breitmann, said he.

Fig.44 Sketch and verse about a Long Room reader c. 1930.

53

In 1909 the Master of the Rolls issued new regulations restricting the admission of "literary" searchers to those who gave evidence of their respectability by applying for tickets on a set form. Applicants for a reader's ticket had to "obtain on a form supplied the recommendation of a person of recognised standing: in the case of those who are of alien status this is obtained through the Foreign Office". The possession of a visiting card was a token of respectability that could be used to gain admission to the reading rooms.

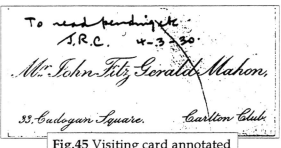

Fig.45 Visiting card annotated with permission to use the search rooms

Between 1909 and 1949, over 12,700 "literary" students were registered for reader's tickets. Jenkinson wrote "there is literally no subject of human interest studied in this Country which might not potentially find illustration in its Public Records". Eventually, the Treasury dropped the imposition of fees on its own records and those levied on legal searches were confined to post-1800 records. Individual departments agreed to further extensions in access to their records and in 1948 the records of the Foreign Office and Colonial Office were opened to 1902.

Production was a carefully regulated procedure - "for every stage in the journey of a Document from Repository to Searcher and back a signature is required .. these stages number eleven .. the reference to the Document must be written by [the Student] or the Officers of the Department four times".The Government Search Room was originally based in a room and lobby behind the Round Room, moving in 1901 to the 'South Room'. After 1945, more seats were provided in the Long Room but by the late 1950s, the total capacity was no more than 100 places and there could be as many as 150 readers a day.

New stimuli towards increased use of the public records were the establishment of the London School of Economics in 1896 and the Institute of Historical Research in 1921; the development of new research degrees in American and British universities and the setting up of many new record-publishing societies. A card index of public records in print was begun in 1912 but fell into desuetude after the 1950s. The launch of the Victoria County History (VCH) at the turn of the century stimulated much work on medieval source material for local history. In the days before female students were allowed to take degrees at the older universities, they provided a source of cheap labour for the systematic mining of certain record classes, recording topographical information on slips that are still used by VCH editors. Their superintendent was a formidable lady with suffragette tendencies who, when quizzed by one of the male assistant keepers as to whether she termed herself a foreman or a forewoman, replied 'A ganger, sir!' Not until 1925 was the first woman assistant keeper appointed.

Repair and Reprographics

As early as 1841, the second *Report* of the Deputy Keeper records the employment of 26 workmen on "repairing and binding". From 1882, a careful register of repairs was kept and by the early years of the twentieth century a team of craftsmen, supervised by one of the assistant keepers, had emerged. New techniques of repair were evolved, drawing on experience from outside, such as the Italian use of silk gauze as a repair material and continental methods of seal repair and moulding. The section also developed its own techniques and even invented a parchment 'roughing' machine in about 1952 which remains in use to the present day. The principles of repair enunciated by Jenkinson, who at one stage was in charge of the Repository and Repairs Department, were "that nothing should be added to or subtracted from the Record, either physically or morally, except where safety requires it: that where material has had to be added it should so far as possible be of the same kind and quality as the original: and that where it is not clear to the eye what has been done in repair this should be the subject of an attached note".

The Office also had a staff of binders, binding some 2,000 volumes a year by 1947. Prefabricated huts were erected on the North Terrace (see fig.24) which, in 1948, came to house the repair workshops. However, conservation staff after the war grew restive under a disciplinary regime that, according to one man, treated them as children to be seen and not heard, regularly inspected standing to attention by their work benches but never asked to discuss repair techniques. Not until 1951 were the Attendant Repairers re-graded as Museum craftsmen.

Fig.46 Repair Staff c. 1912 and c. 1935.

The provision of reprographic services began in a limited way in 1891 when the office established a temporary studio on site for use by approved applicants who wished to photograph documents. Photographic work was subsequently contracted out to a private firm, Monger and Marchant, who were based near Chancery Lane. During the First World War, a photographic studio was set up in the basement of the Chancery Lane building for the filming of war diaries and other military records. In 1920 one of the photostat machines that had been used by the Canadian military historical unit was hired out to Monger and Marchant, who paid for the electricity they used and charged the Office 2s 6d per sheet. This basic arrangement continued until 1944.

In 1928, the Library of Congress installed a second machine to copy records of American interest. This machine came into the possession of the Office and was eventually used for both certified copies i.e. official copies that were legally admissible documents and uncertified copies i.e. copies made for private study purposes, in what Jenkinson calls "a change almost revolutionary if one bears in mind the importance assigned to the making of Office Copies by the Staff in the early organisation of the Department". Not until 1942 did the Office accept that photostats could be used for certified copies and then only because of the wartime staff shortage. In 1940, the Library of Congress and University Microfilms of Michigan installed a microfilm camera at Chancery Lane "the scheme being primarily to guard against some of the effects of bombing by micro photographing large series of Documents here and elsewhere in England and depositing the film at Washington". Camera operators were drawn from the Repairers. As part of the agreement, one of the microfilm cameras was to be handed over to the Office at the end of the exercise and thus the internal Reprographics operation was born. After 1945, large scale microfilming orders for Australia and Canada boosted the size of the Photographic Section and the range of services it was able to offer to the public.

War

Shortly after the outbreak of the First World War, concern was expressed as to the possible effects of aerial bombardment of the building and certain records, including Domesday Book, were eventually evacuated to Bodmin prison and to the Post Office underground railway. In October 1917, a shell fragment actually

Fig.47 Growing our Food in Chancery Lane c.1917. Hubert Hall was then the Resident Officer. An assistant keeper remained on site overnight until December 1977 in case any documents were urgently required by a government department.

penetrated the glass roof of the Round Room. A number of staff joined up and seven were killed, one on the first day of the Battle of the Somme.

As early as 1933 contingency plans had been drawn up for the evacuation of public records from London in the event of war. It was even suggested that railway trains be used to store the records so that they could always be quickly moved away from danger. In 1938, the Office was offered parts of a disused prison at Shepton Mallet and a workhouse at Market Harborough. Records began to move there in August 1939 and then also to Belvoir Castle, Haddon Hall, Culham College, Clandon Park House and Grittleton House. Eventually, half a million records were evacuated. Each store had a small staff and the war provided an opportunity to carry out editorial work on the evacuated records. In London, records were moved to the lower floors of the Chancery Lane repository. Of the search rooms, originally closed down, the Long Room reopened with a limited service.

Fig.48 L C Hector (far right) with records evacuated to Haddon Hall. PRO 18/5.

A number of incendiary bombs fell on the building but none did serious damage, although the Office narrowly escaped when much of Fetter Lane was devastated in 1941. The Deputy Keeper reported that on some nights it was possible "to read a newspaper in the glare of neighbouring fires".

Fig.49 View from Fleet Street,
30 December 1940. PRO 50/59.

About one quarter of the Office's 120 staff were called up for national service. Some assistant keepers undertook war diary analysis for the War Office Historical Section, which took over part of the Chancery Lane building. Hilary Jenkinson became official Adviser on Archives to the War Office, identifying collections in Italy and Germany that Allied Forces were to safeguard. He became Deputy Keeper in 1947 and in the dark days of the Cold War period, he was sharply to contrast the role of the Archivist as a "devotee of Truth" with that of the Propagandist.

Fig.50 PRO staff ready for any eventuality c. 1939. PRO 50/ 59. Note the unimpeded view of the re-erected medieval arch from the Rolls Chapel in the centre.

Expansion to other sites

In the period of retrenchment after the end of the First World War, the Treasury was not willing to provide funds either for a new building or extension on the Chancery Lane site. However the Chancery Lane repository was now full and there was a major new problem in holding the records generated by the needs

59

of wartime administration, pending their review. An inter-departmental committee of representatives of the Treasury, Office of Works and Public Record Office was established in 1919 to review the Office's long-term needs. As a temporary expedient, the disused county gaol at Cambridge was taken over as a record store. That was exchanged for Canterbury gaol in 1929, later to be evacuated in 1941-42. The Committee recommended expanding the Office by purchasing part of the adjoining Clifford's Inn and then taking over the adjacent St. Dunstan's House site when its lease reverted to the Crown in 1966. The Treasury was sceptical about the long-term future of the congested Chancery Lane site and felt that it would be more sensible to transfer the whole Office to the suburbs, possibly Acton. Extending the Chancery Lane building east and south to create a rectangular complex was again under discussion in 1938 but the outbreak of war left these plans stillborn.

The Second World War expanded the civil service bureaucracy and multiplied the generation of records which would clearly cause difficulties after the war ended. In 1943 the Master of the Rolls set up a small committee to look into the problem which identified a three-stage life-cycle for the record - current, semi-current and selection for permanent preservation. In the semi-current phase, departments needed somewhere to deposit files that were only needed for occasional reference and at this stage they could be weeded. The committee recommended the establishment of a 'Limbo' repository to accommodate such records, managed by the Public Record Office. By 1948, a number of stations on an unfinished Underground railway line had been taken over for this purpose, housing over 160,000 feet of records, almost as much as space as was provided by the Chancery Lane building. Eventually tube shelters at Furnival Street, Goodge Street, Belsize Park, Camden Town, Clapham North, Clapham Common and Stockwell were taken over, as well as a disused factory at Yeading and further sites in Grosvenor Road and Leake Street. They were cleared between 1950 and 1964 after a former Royal Ordnance Factory at Hayes was taken over in 1950 as a 'limbo' repository for semi-current records. By 1956 this housed over half a million feet of records. In 1951, a branch repository was opened at Ashridge Park in Hertfordshire, with a public search room. Records were stored there until 1980 when they were transferred to the Office's new building at Kew. Alarmed by the spiralling costs of record storage in departments, the Treasury commissioned an Organisation and Methods survey into how departments transferred records to the PRO. Completed in 1951, this revealed that quarter of a million feet of records housed in departments merited immediate destruction but that records destined for permanent preservation were likely to more than double the PRO's existing holdings. Churchill himself, struck by ever-rising expenditure on filing cabinets, authorised the establishment of a Committee on Departmental Records.

The Grigg Report

The Committee on Departmental Records under Sir James Grigg, whose report was published in 1954 (Cmd 9163), recommended that departmental records be reviewed twice, once for their continued administrative utility, at which stage it was estimated that 50-90% could be destroyed, and again at 25 years when historical criteria should be taken into account. Each department should have its own record officer. A Records Administration Department was established and new inspecting officer posts created. Grigg also recommended that the Public Records Acts of the nineteenth century were out-dated and should be repealed and that a uniform 50-year closure period should be introduced, which was intended to keep the papers of officials closed within their lifetimes. Commenting on the draft report, the historian Sir Llewellyn Woodward thought this reasonable but questioned whether the detailed annexes to Cabinet minutes should be made available as "I don't feel altogether certain that the fact that they will be open even after 50 years may not have a bad effect on the freedom of Cabinet discussion". He also argued that "a high proportion of the number of applicants to read 'closed' papers are not genuine scholars, but persons wanting to get at the material in order to attack HM Government and British policy generally". In the event, the Lord Chancellor, who was to become the minister responsible for the public records, was empowered to vary the closure period, up or down, if a case was made by the creating department.

The Public Records Act of 1958 and the move to Kew

The Public Records Acts, 1958 and 1967

he 1958 Act created a new office of Keeper of the Public Records to take charge of the Public Record Office under the Lord Chancellor. Records selected for permanent preservation were to be transferred not later than 30 years after their creation to the Office or to an approved place of deposit, such as the India Office Library for the records of the British administration of India, or local authority record offices for records of quarter sessions, hospital boards etc. In dealing with other government departments, its role remained co-ordinating and supervisory, rather than regulatory. As the Keeper's Report for 1972 later noted "it can formulate procedures and standards for the guidance of departments in managing their records, but it had no power itself to coerce or bring sanctions to bear on laggard departments". Records were to be open to public inspection 50 years after the last date on the file. The 1958 Act also provided for the establishment of an Advisory Council "to advise the Lord Chancellor on matters concerning public records in general and, in particular, on those aspects of the work of the Public Record Office which affect members of the public who make use of the facilities". In 1960, the first Cabinet Office records were transferred to the Office, as recommended by the Grigg Report, with a normal 50-year closure period, unless disclosure was deemed to be "contrary to the public interest".

In 1964, the Advisory Council recommended a 40-year closure period and more liberal access to closed records, transmitting the views of "many scholars of repute and standing" who wanted it reduced to 30 years and who believed that "departments are far too rigid and unbending, and refuse permission to see documents which could well be shown without injury to the public interest at all". The Council argued that "there are other countries which are more liberal in some respects than this country in giving access to their records. In consequence historians using those sources - without the benefit of ours - are liable to present a picture of recent events which may be incomplete and unbalanced. It would be a valuable corrective if historians could have freer access than at present to our records". The closure period was reduced to 30 years by the Public Records Act of 1967.

Staff and Readers

In 1959, there were 169 staff in post but shortages of lower paid repair staff and repository assistants who proved more difficult to recruit in periods of full employment. There was a similar staffing crisis in the early 1970s. By 1960, the authorised complement had been increased to 188 and in 1963, there were 204 staff in post. Reflecting the militancy of the times, in August 1974 there was a strike which closed the search rooms for six days.

The relative proportion of staff in curatorial grades continued to fall and the Advisory Council noted in 1973 that "the number of Assistant Keepers in the Office is almost the same as it was in the 1920s. We think this is a deplorable situation". It was noted that between 1925 and 1930, every one of the 22 assistant keepers was doing some editorial work on medieval records and 16 volumes of medieval record publications were produced. In contrast, 1967 to 1972 saw only three assistant keepers out of 23 doing medieval work and the publication of five medieval titles. A Medieval Sub-Group of the Publications Committee warned that the Office was in danger of losing "the position that it has always had as a centre of medieval scholarship". Yet was this what the Office existed for ? After 1958, assistant keepers were no longer recruited predominantly from medievalists, but until the 1980s, rarely from holders of professional archival qualifications. One assistant keeper recalls that "at one time the PRO was extremely precious in distancing itself from the emerging profession of 'archivist' (i.e. local archivist) to the extent that (after Jenkinson had retired) the term itself was anathema within the hallowed walls".

Fig.51 John Watkins and Sheila Hayward in the Office Library at Chancery Lane, 1995.

One assistant keeper recalls that "the library at Chancery Lane offered some of the facilities, and disadvantages, of a common room. It was generally reckoned inadvisable to go there after 3.30 pm, because the presence of L C Hector (an indefatigable raconteur) made it likely that one would miss one's train home". The Library with its strong collection of works on medieval history and local record society publications was an important scholarly resource, albeit with a very idiosyncratic cataloguing system and occasional curiosities, such as novels written by members of staff.

From the late 1960s, a number of executive officers were promoted to curatorial grades. Alfred Mabbs, who had joined the Office in 1938 as a clerical officer, was elevated to the keepership itself in 1978, "from Limbo to Olympus" as one of his colleagues put it.

The increasing public demand for microfilm and photographic copies led to huge expansion in the reprographic operation which had 65 staff by 1969. The Office also wanted to provide microform substitutes in the reading rooms for preservation purposes. The 1971 Keeper's *Report* stated that "the inferior quality of much wartime paper and the vulnerability of many modern departmental files to wear and tear are growing problems, and the substitution of photocopies, whether in microform or facsimile, is frequently a cheaper and more practical alternative to documentary repair". By 1971, the Microfilm Library held 3.1 million feet of film.

Fig.52 Reprographic staff at Chancery Lane c. 1989 (l. to r.) - Donna Rochester, Marion Moka, Mona Singh, Simon Brown, Rajpatie Budhai, Alan Jensen and Fiona Prothero. The room is a converted strongroom. Note the original small thick panes of glass in cast-iron frames.

Staff in Conservation were no longer willing to accept the rigid disciplines of the 1940s and 50s. Despite a ban on the use of radios in office hours, transistor radio sets were built into concealed containers with external switches that could be switched off at a moment's notice. More emphasis was placed on professional training and some conservators were sent on introductory chemistry courses at Camberwell School of Arts and Crafts. Something of a divide emerged between new recruits with paper qualifications and those who had effectively served craft apprenticeships within the Office, albeit on a somewhat *ad hoc* basis. J J New, who served for many years as Foreman of the Conservation Section, gained an international reputation as a craftsman and teacher.

Fig.53 Repository staff in the Long Room c. 1960 (l. to r.) - Mr Wingfield, unknown, Mr Coleman, Mr Lea. Brown dust jackets, collar and tie were a compulsory uniform.

65

The appointment of S S Wilson as Keeper in October 1960, the man in the words of John Cantwell "earmarked in the 50s for the job, as the Treasury saw it, of dragging the PRO into the twentieth century", heralded a new interest in statistical analysis. Statistics and readership surveys were used against his traditionalist critics to highlight the predominant use by readers of modern and early modern sources rather than medieval ones. Between December 1960 and August 1961, all readers were invited to complete a questionnaire. About one in eight did so, and the 400 returns comprised 54 UK university teachers, 38 foreign university teachers, 46 teachers, 72 research students, 26 "record agents, archivists, genealogists etc." and 164 "other". They asked for more assistance for new readers, longer opening hours, more space, better finding aids, faster document production and a quicker photographic service. In 1963 a Rank Xerox 914 copier was introduced to provide a "while-you-wait" service at 1s. a sheet. Usage of records by each group was further analysed in 1965, as the following extract from the Keeper's *Report* of that year shows:

In the following table Col. 1 shows the percentage of readers with 3-year tickets current in 1965; Col. 2 shows the percentage of requisitions of documents in 1965 by that group.

			% of readers	% of documents	
U.K. University teachers ...	...		7	10	
Students	...	...	13	23	
School teachers	...	...	...	9	4
Lawyers	...	...	3	1	
Record agents	...	...	...	2	8
Writers	...	...	2	3	
Others	...	...	45	24	
Readers from overseas	...	...	19	27	
			100	100	
Actual		...	7,425	134,000	

(In addition 10,300 documents were produced in 1965 to applicants for temporary tickets).

A search room was opened in 1970 for the consultation of wills, inventories and other probate records, formerly made available in the Principal Probate Registry, which contributed to the 9% surge in attendance between 1970 and 1971, to 85,000 readers consulting 306,000 documents a year. The accelerated opening of records from the Second World War in 1972 pushed these figures up again to 97,000 and 316,200 respectively.

In 1970, a market research company was brought in to carry out a reader survey . It found that 70% were students or academics; 13% professional researchers; 7% central or local government officers and the remaining 10% "people in a wide range of occupations as well as retired persons and housewives pursuing research as a hobby". Nearly half (49%) were from the London area and 43% were regular users. Of the 20% who were first time users, 94% anticipated a return visit. Over a third (34%) were pursuing genealogical research. Most readers (87%) needed to consult search room staff and a third (32%) experienced "some difficulty in using the search room lists and indexes". Only 7% objected to proposals for moving records to a new site at Kew. The Office's readership had become increasingly cosmopolitan. Academic historians and post-graduate researchers were still very significant, but numbers were swelled by an ever rising tide of family historians, which in turn had implications for search room staffing. The assistant keepers came to be diverted more from search room duty to editorial work on finding aids. Writing in 1993, John Cantwell warned of the danger that the PRO "should, by over-responding as it were, to the mass market, damage its long-standing links with the academic community". However, all types of user, new and old alike, have legitimate needs that must be appropriately balanced in the competition for resources. As the Keeper's *Report* for 1972 pointed out, the Office had a dual role as "a department providing a common service to other Government departments and an institution providing the public with a service of a kind which caters for the needs of a great variety of users. In discharging its role of providing the best possible service to government and public the Office has the difficult task of striking the right balance between interests which sometimes conflict with each other. In so doing it can only be guided by what it conceives to be broadly the public interest". It defined the Office's broad aims as :

"a)   to preserve records of permanent value for research and administrative purposes, and make them available for these purposes;

b)   to ensure that other records are kept for as long as they are needed and are then destroyed;

c)   to oversee the selection of records to these ends;

d)   to provide advice on record matters generally."

By 1962, the Search Department was receiving 5,000 letters of enquiry from the public a year, half of which were genealogical and mainly relating to census returns or service records. By 1972, the Office was receiving 18,000 letters of enquiry, including orders for copies, a year. Official policy remained that queries involving extensive searches could not be undertaken as "it is inappropriate that at public expense extended and lengthy searches - which may often be unproductive - should be made to further the researches of private individuals". The enquirer was to be recommended to employ a record agent. Record agents had long played a vital role in this respect, in the words of Roger Ellis forming "that learned and devoted, and all too little regarded, body of men and women who have for so long been the mainstay of historical research". Paid searches "within reasonable limits" were introduced in 1965, on pre-payment of £3, but it was stated that the Office "will for the time being continue to make certain short searches without charge, especially where the query appears to be of a general historical nature".

In 1912, the Census Returns for 1841 and 1851, which had been under threat of destruction, were deposited in the Office so that official searches could be made for the ages of applicants for the new old age pensions, first introduced in 1909. Until 1952, fees were levied on their inspection. In 1964 the census returns for 1841, 1851 and 1861 were microfilmed and thereafter microfilm copies were made available for local libraries to purchase. These microfilms were to become the single most popular source used by the public, so popular that in June 1971 the Census search rooms in Portugal Street were opened on Saturdays for "many amateur genealogists and other users whose only free time was on Saturday" although this ceased in 1976 after a dispute with staff over terms and conditions of their transfer to the new Kew Office. In 1990, microfilm search rooms for census returns were opened in the basement of Chancery Lane, using converted strong room accommodation, and the Saturday service was resumed in 1994.

Fig.54 Entrance to the Census Rooms at Chancery Lane, 1995.

Selection, Publication and Listing

At its first meeting in 1959, the Advisory Council had called for the publication of lists and indexes and established a Publication Committee, similar to the former Consultative Committee on Publication which last met in 1957, on which a number of university historians sat. Record publication, the Committee felt, "should be a public service and the question of demand should play no part in determining prices". It also wished that "some system can be devised by which individual scholars may be permitted to purchase copies of texts and calendars directly bearing on their studies at reduced prices from the Public Record Office itself". In 1961, it called for more emphasis on the period after 1800 and "greater use .. of modern methods of reproduction by way of microfilm and microcard in lieu of printing", proposing that the Memoranda Rolls of the Exchequer (down to 1307) be published on microfilm, rather than as a printed edition, but with a printed index of persons and places to accompany it. The Office responded to this by publishing in 1962, small editions of micro-opaque cards, of seventeenth-century Privy Council registers, eighteenth-century Treasury minute books and nineteenth-century Colonial Office records.

Entrance to the Census Rooms at Chancery Lane, 1995. In 1964, past publication achievements were surveyed and it was calculated that, between them, the Record Commissions, Public Record Office and Rolls Series had produced 1,000 volumes "with at least two major series covering each year from 1200-1750; overall, the average coverage for each year is about 800 pages of text, with 20,000 index entries". However, the demand for many texts and calendars was now too small to justify the costs of producing them, estimated as "at least two years full-time editorial work for each volume .. not less than £5,000". Nonetheless, the Kraus-Thomson Organisation Ltd found it worthwhile to re-issue many out-of-print texts and calendars, under licence from HMSO, and in 1972 agreement was reached with the same organisation for the joint publication of public records "in which each party shares costs and, ultimately, profits". More emphasis was placed on producing handbooks to twentieth-century source material, such as *Records of Interest to Social Scientists 1919-1939* which was compiled by two external editors, funded by the Social Science Research Council, and published in 1971.

In 1965, the Office supported the formation of an unofficial List and Index Society to reproduce the unpublished class lists in the search rooms as they stood and without further editing. Institutional members of the Society contracted to buy all its publications but private members could be selective. The choice of volumes to be published was made on the basis of recommendations by the members themselves. By 1969, 48 volumes had been produced for the 228 institutional and 112 private subscribers. A new series of Museum pamphlets was launched in 1972, with facsimiles of selected documents to illustrate a particular theme, set in their historical context.

One of the most difficult problems facing those responsible for the selection of records was that of bulky case files created by the ever expanding influence of central government in the nineteenth and twentieth centuries over the lives of the private citizen. A committee was established to look into the representative sampling of particular instance papers, such as personal records of members of the armed forces, as "they contain a great wealth of facts about particular persons, firms, institutions and the like, but the immense bulk of paper involved makes it imperative to ascertain most carefully the minimum quantity which it is essential to keep for the purpose of research". The Grigg Report had concluded that "no attempt should be made to keep in the PRO records which would not otherwise be preserved, solely because they contain information which might be useful for genealogical or biographical purposes". This view was endorsed by the Advisory Council in 1965 which recommended that "departments maintaining personal and individual records of large groups of the population (including the basic records of service in the armed forces since 1900) should not preserve them after their administrative usefulness is exhausted. We would, however, suggest that in suitable cases a statistical sample be kept". The application of this policy to the Crew Lists and Agreements for 1853-1913, held by the Registrar General of Shipping and Seamen, led to much public criticism of the Office. Only a 10% statistical sample for the period 1861-1913 and documents relating to "noteworthy" ships were eventually retained by the PRO. It is a problem that has not yet been satisfactorily resolved. In 1973, the Advisory Council noted that "the use of magnetic tape in place of a traditional medium offers the possibility of preserving large quantities of information in a form which is relatively compact, and which is also capable of further processing for research purposes" which might allow for their recommendation of 1965 to be revised.

The Keeper's *Report* for 1964 considered for the first time the possibility of a computerised index, to index the estimated 30 million names in pre-1875 ''Chancery Proceedings''. It envisaged a team of 30 indexers working for 20 years at a cost of £45,000 p.a. and a "machine system for retrieving information" at a cost of £20,000 p.a., but concluded that even if the number of productions from these classes rose ten-fold as a result, the average cost of 45s. per search could not be justified "to facilitate a relatively narrow demand". In 1968, it was announced that a working party would probably be set up to look at "the problems of selection for permanent preservation of records processed by computers and the documentation associated with their use". In 1975, discussions opened with the Social Science Research Council Data Archive at Essex University on a possible agency service for the conversion and duplication of machine-readable records.

In 1971, a pilot project for processing information about records at class level, based on the INSPEC system developed by the Institution of Electrical Engineers to produce abstracts of journals and indexes, was begun. Known as PROSPEC, it was intended to provide a database from which could be taken a new *Guide to Departmental Records* in three editions a year; repository location lists; catalogues of search room lists and an annual catalogue of the microfilm library. It was even suggested that PROSPEC might be expanded and made available to other record offices in the country.

Fig.55 Assistant keeper David Crook at work in A23, 1995.

In 1969, a project to sort hitherto unsorted Chancery files and reunite them with stray documents that were previously assigned to other classes began. "In the great Chancery Files sort of the early 1970s, one editorial assistant with big feet was used to get recalcitrant files into standard size boxes .. when he wasn't practising archery by using rubber bands to fire parchment needles on to the Law Society roof." Experiments were made in 1970-71 with the use of "selected long term prisoners in HM Prisons" for indexing records, including street indexes to the census returns. "One prisoner who had been working on records was, after release on parole, employed for some months as an editor, working under the supervision of a probation officer."

The Accommodation Crisis and the Move to Kew

Pressure on space at the Chancery Lane site became ever more acute. In 1961, a large strongroom directly above the Long Room, known as the Rolls Room, which had been used for the storage of Chancery enrolments, was converted into a 40-seat reading room, despite the fact that public access was confined to a narrow spiral staircase which posed problems for elderly or disabled readers. The gain was offset by the loss of ten seats in South Room which was divided into a waiting room and room for the sorting and packing of records. The Rolls Room subsequently became a microfilm reading room used mainly for registered copy wills and death duty records.

Fig.56 The Rolls Room, formerly the Copying Office, before conversion to a reading room in 1961.

More strongrooms were converted into reading rooms known as the North Room and Annexe in 1967 which provided another 40 places. Development of the St. Dunstan's House site with a tower block that included a 250-seat reading room was again under discussion in 1960 and when this was abandoned, a search room on the roof of the existing Chancery Lane building, concealed by the parapets, was suggested. By 1965, there were regularly over 200 readers a day for 120 places available in the reading rooms and the Keeper's *Report* for that year noted that "on occasions the crowding was acute with risk of damage to the documents". Readers from the London area were advised not to come in during the summer. The Advisory Council complained that "the scarcity of accommodation is not only having an adverse effect upon the work of senior scholars but is also calculated to discourage research". In 1967 a 20-seat search room was opened on the Hayes site "for groups of students wishing to make an intensive study of classes of modern records not in public demand" and at Chancery Lane, the conversion of more strongroom accommodation increased the seating to 160 places. The introduction of the 30-year rule in January 1968 contributed to a 25% increase in the number of readers using the search rooms in that year. As another temporary stop-gap in 1968, a search room with fifty seats for consulting census returns on microfilm was opened in the Land Registry building in nearby Portugal Street. The Conservation Department also moved there and two more search rooms, known as the East and West Rooms, were opened there in 1969-1970, mainly for users of Cabinet, Foreign Office and Colonial Office records. By then, the three search rooms at Portugal Street provided as many seats as the main Chancery Lane building but it was clear that another site would have to be found for the ever mounting volume of accessions. In 1972, the Public Record Office took over responsibility from British Rail for the 15,000 feet of records of the British Transport Historical Record Office, mainly records of the pre-nationalised railway companies, and originally destined for the new Railway Museum at York. It took over their existing site at Porchester House, Paddington which operated as an out-station until the records were transferred to Kew in 1977. In the same year (1972) nearly 700 classes of records of the Second World War were given accelerated opening.

In 1966, it was estimated that by the year 2000, accommodation for 900 readers inspecting 4000 documents a day would be needed. Development of the St. Dunstan's House site might achieve this, but the cellular construction of the Chancery Lane building meant that mechanical handling systems could never be successfully used in the repository and many more repository staff would therefore have to be recruited to service them. In 1963, a system of pneumatic tubes was introduced to transmit tickets ordering documents from the search rooms to the repository floors. This reduced average production times from 32 minutes to 24, but Chancery Lane, as John Cantwell admits, was "ill-designed to cope with the massive increase in productions which gathered pace from the 1960s".

Further inspection of the St. Dunstan's site proved its inadequacy and in 1969 the Advisory Council concluded that "any site in central London would probably not be large enough to permit expansion after the year 2000", but that any new site "should be in the London area, accessible by frequent public transport".

Fig.57 Production difficulties on A Floor.

In 1969, it was decided to build a new repository for departmental records on part of the crown estate off Ruskin Avenue, Kew. It was to have a mechanical document delivery system and two large reading rooms, each with 248 seats and closed circuit TV cameras for more efficient invigilation. The Advisory Council noted that the Kew site would add about one hour to readers' travelling time but that "after weighing all the advantages and disadvantages, we are convinced that the Ruskin Avenue site is the best available and, in view of the urgent needs of the Public Record Office, that any further delay caused by a search for possible alternatives could not be justified". It called for extended opening hours to compensate for the extra travelling time. Work began in 1973 and the new office was completed at a cost of £8 million in 1977, with some 69 miles of shelving in large open-plan air-conditioned repositories where small electric cars could be used to fetch and carry documents to a central continuously moving 'paternoster' conveyor system. In his novel *Kew for Murder* (Robert Hale, 1984), Charles Cruickshank was later to portray the fictitious delivery of a corpse in the paternoster system to a royal visitor touring the Kew building. Following consultation with users, the records transferred to Kew were those of "modern" government departments, mostly post-1782 but including records of older departments such as Treasury, Admiralty and War Office which went back to the sixteenth century and even earlier. The move of over 2.5 million documents began in May 1977 and took six months. The reading rooms at Kew opened to the public on 17 October 1977.

Medieval records, state papers before 1782, legal records up to the present day and census returns on microfilm remained in central London. Also transferred to Kew was the Records Administration Division which, from 1975, had had to be out-housed at Hanover Square in the West End. A computerised document ordering system called PROMPT was introduced at Kew which required readers to key in their ticket number, seat number and the reference of the documents they wished to order, instead of filling in paper tickets. Unless the reference typed in was incorrect or the document was not available, in which case an appropriate message appeared upon the screen, a two-part ticket would then be printed out on the appropriate repository floor. One part of the ticket would then be put in place of the document on shelf and the other part went down to the reading room with the document. The system was later (1985) extended to Chancery Lane, replacing the pneumatic tube system. When the computerised ordering system, which depended on a land line to Kew, broke down, a not infrequent sight by the lift shaft near the Round Room was a cardboard wallet on the end of a long piece of string that was used like a fishing line to haul up paper tickets to the appropriate repository floor. There was also an attempt to introduce electric cars but driving them proved hazardous in Chancery Lane's narrow corridors and none could enter into the strongrooms. Another problem was the lack of air conditioning at Chancery Lane which helped to promote periodic outbreaks of mildew. Ventilation in the strongrooms depended on opening and shutting windows under the guidance of a hygrometer, no small task if there were 140 rooms each with 4-8 windows.

Fig.58 Tom Loft producing documents on A floor, 1995.

Fig.59 B floor corridor, 1995. Note the electric cars which proved wholly impractical at Chancery Lane.

Writing in 1983, Michael Moss criticised the split of records between Chancery Lane, Hayes and Kew, particularly for historians using departmental records at Kew and discovering that related legal papers then had to be seen at Chancery Lane or ordered from Hayes, which could take three days. The answer, in his view, was to close Chancery Lane and shift its records and staff to Kew. This is not a view with which the medieval historian using Chancery Lane records in conjunction with related material at the British Library would necessarily sympathise, but the attraction of bringing together most of the public records on the same site, for the first time since the 1920s, ultimately prevailed. By the late 1980s, with new accessions coming in at a rate of about a mile a year, the Kew building also proved inadequate for the Office's needs and it was decided to add another new building, popularly known as 'New PRO' to the old. Work was completed in 1996. It was decided to close the Chancery Lane Office and transfer all original records held there to Kew. This operation was very smoothly carried out, with minimum disruption to readers, in 1995-1996. At the time of writing (October 1996) the Government is actively looking for a suitable use for the Chancery Lane building.

The Closure of Chancery Lane

Fig.60 William Stockting inspecting records in the Tower, boxed for transfer to Kew, 1995.

In 1995-1996, elements of continuity with the Chancery Lane site were incorporated into the approach to the new building at Kew. The decorative ironwork on the main gate represents medieval tally sticks; slate shelves from Chancery Lane were used as paving and wall decoration in the gardens; the rose known as "Conqueror's Gold" that had been created by Harkness of Hitchin to mark the 900th anniversary of Domesday Book and planted at Chancery Lane was moved to the circular plot before the main entrance; lead cisterns dated 1718 and 1724 originally from houses which had fronted Chancery Lane (nos 6 and 7), were placed on either side of the new public entrance.

The last office-keeper of the Chancery Lane building was moved to poetry, in verse showing the depth of feeling that an ordinary member of staff felt for the resonance of the site.

GOODBYE CHANCERY LANE

Imposing as ever, but without its heart,
The building stands in Chancery Lane,
For now it is lonely, quiet and sad,
It shall never be the same again.

Ghosts may drift through the empty rooms,
Like a memory of the past that dies,
But some of us will never forget
The great part it has played in our lives.

The documents have all been removed,
No more treasures behind those heavy doors,
Now a tranquil silence pervades the air,
As voices no longer echo along the floors.

The empty shelves mock the Round Room,
In the Long Room the tables have gone,
The Rolls Room is grey and lifeless,
Where once so much research was done.

The Rolls Chapel is empty too,
But for the brooding tombs,
Whose occupants keep a watchful eye,
On the abandoned reading rooms.

So the lights have been extinguished,
The old building stands empty and alone,
Only people's memories will keep it alive,
Now the PRO has departed its home.

© Alan Jensen 1996

The late twentieth-century user of Chancery Lane would still recognise the initial impression of one nineteenth-century editor, J S Brewer, of "a number of narrow passages flagged with brick; iron doors to the right and left, marked with cabalistic numerals, and furnished with small circular ventilators [which] divide these passages with geometrical exactness". Designed to intimidate, it intimidates still and, in an era of more open government, perhaps it carried that message across too strongly to survive. Nonetheless for many of those who successfully penetrated to its heart, as readers or as members of staff, a deep and sentimental affection developed for its labyrinthine corridors and "mechanical" Gothic details. The shining white neo-tudor towers of Chancery Lane, sparkling in the sun against a pale blue sky or more typically starkly silhouetted against slate grey, will forever conjure up for them a romantic inspiration of the Muse of History.

Fig.61 "Coffins' awaiting transfer to Kew.